LITURGIES
with young people

EDITED BY DONAL NEARY SJ

First published in 2017 by Messenger Publications

ISBN 978 1 910248 85 0

Designed by Messenger Publications Design Department
Typeset in Bembo and Futura
Printed by Nicholson & Bass Ltd

Messenger Publications,
37 Lower Leeson Street, Dublin D02 W938
www.messenger.ie

FOREWORD

Pope Francis reminds us that by its very nature the liturgy is 'popular' and not 'clerical'. It is an action 'for the people but also of the people'. (Address during National Liturgical Week, Italy, 24 August 2017.)

I welcome the publication of *Liturgies with Young People*. While drawing on the editor's previous material, this book, with its many new reflections and prayers, is up to date in its outreach to a new generation, and is the fruit of the work of catechists and chaplains currently working in our schools who have contributed to its make-up.

The content may be used either for Mass, or with adaptation, for non-Eucharistic liturgies and prayer services, and takes into account the spiritual development and interest of this age group. The reflections and ideas within can be easily adapted to the age, and the level of understanding of the group.

The themes are also inclusive of the interest and different backgrounds of our school pupils, here again in tune with the Pope's approach to liturgy: 'The Church in prayer gathers all those whose hearts listen to the gospel, without excluding anyone. The small and the great are called, as are the rich and the poor, children and old people, the healthy and the sick, the just and sinners. The "popular" reach of Liturgy reminds us that it is inclusive and not exclusive'.

I am confident that those working in faith formation with young people, in schools, parishes and elsewhere will find here plenty of material and ideas for prayer and liturgy with our young people. In wishing this book well, I pay tribute to the work of the many chaplains and religion teachers in our schools who, after their parents, and with their parish, are such important influences in the faith life of each new generation.

+Eamon Martin, Archbishop of Armagh

ACKNOWLEDGEMENTS

Thanks to The Columba Press for permission to use material from the editor's previous publications.

The editor thanks the chaplains and teachers who contributed from their material composed for use in schools: Ronan Barry, Gráinne Delaney, Celine Donohoe, Linda Kiely, John McHugh and Elaine O'Sullivan. Much of the content is theirs and many of the reflections.
All uncredited reflections are either by the editor or the contributors, with some adaptation. While they were very much in an essential role during the preparation of the book, the editor takes responsibility for the final product. Thanks also to the staff of Messenger Publications for editorial assistance and design, for encouragement and their publicity for the book.

The editor also thanks, in acknowledgement:
Michael Drumm and Tom Gunning for their reflection (p.17)
Joy Cowley for Magnificat (p.35)
Joy Mitchell for 'you can be more than you dreamed' (p.81)
Roy Lessin for the reflection 'Just think, you're not here by chance' (p.86)
'Education for Justice' for their Diversity Blessing (p.98)
and Prayer for Refugees (p.49)
Joe Seremane for 'A prayer from Africa' (p.112)

Editor: Donal Neary SJ is presently editor of *The Sacred Heart Messenger*, and formerly chaplain in the Mater Dei Institute of Education and parish priest at Gardiner Street parish, Dublin. His first book, *The Calm beneath the Storm* (Veritas 1983), proved a very popular choice among second level students, as did many of his books for prayer in Advent, Lent and Easter, which were published by The Columba Press. His latest series, *Gospel Reflections for Sundays of Years A, B and C*, was published by Messenger Publications. He also contributes to www.sacredspace.ie and writes the weekly reflection for the Logos Missalette.

CONTENTS

1. BEGINNING THE SCHOOL YEAR

PREPARATION

Create a prayer space in your classroom with different symbols representing school life (e.g. a book, a football or basketball, a school journal, the Bible, the school mission statement or icon of your founder, a cross). Light a candle at the centre of the space. Ask each of the students to pray for one gift that they will need during this school year. Ask them to write it on a 'post-it' and gather these words in a basket. Add them to your prayer space. Conclude this preparation with a moment of silence. As you leave for your school liturgy, bring these prayerful words to be added to the other student's words.

or

Photographs might be taken of work going on in different classes, students at lunchtime, sports and different activities. Print them out and arrange and cut them to fit into the shape of a body – big enough to be seen by all at the service. It could be displayed in the school somewhere afterwards. Alternatively, get a group of students to construct something out of Lego using one brick for every student in the school – the idea being that together we can be a support for each other and we have a good foundation for the year to come.

INTRODUCTION

As we begin our school year we pray for each other, and for the whole school. We'll be asking God's help with our study, our friendships, our sport, our hobbies and with everything that is part of our school.

We might feel a bit afraid of the coming year, especially if it's an exam year, or if we feel we don't get on too well in the class. We might also feel very confident and glad to start again. No matter what, we put ourselves before God and ask his help in the coming year.

PENITENTIAL RITE

As we begin, we ask God's forgiveness for our faults and failings, for our sinfulness and particularly for ways in which we needlessly hurt each other:

You have come to bring us the life of love. **Lord have mercy.**

You have come to bring us the light of truth. **Christ have mercy**.

You plead for us at the right hand of God our Father. **Lord have mercy**.

OPENING PRAYER

Help us, Lord, at the beginning of our school year.
Help us in our work and in our friendships.
We ask this through Christ our Lord. Amen.

FIRST READING

1 Chronicles 28:20

A wish for the coming year.

A reading from the first book of the Chronicles.

David also said to Solomon his son, 'Be strong and courageous, and do the work. Do not be afraid or discouraged, for the Lord God, my God, is with you. He will not fail you or forsake you until all the work is finished.'

The word of the Lord.

RESPONSORIAL PSALM

Psalm 36

A prayer of trust for the coming year.

Response: be our help, Lord God, in the days to come.

If you trust in the Lord and do good,
then you will live in the land and be secure.
If you find your delight in the Lord,
he will grant your heart's desire. **R.**
Commit your life to the Lord,
trust in him and he will act,
so that your justice beaks forth like the light,
and your cause like the noon day sun. **R.**

GOSPEL READING

Mark 4:35-41

When we look to another year, we don't know what's in store; will it be a happy year, a difficult one? The gospel is a story of trusting in the presence of Jesus as he was present in the apostles' rough times, so he is present always with us.

A reading from the holy Gospel according to Mark.

With the coming of evening that same day, he said to them, 'Let us cross over to the other side.' And leaving the crowd behind they took him, just as he was, in the boat; and there were other boats with him. Then it began to blow a great gale and the waves were breaking into the boat so that it was almost swamped. But he was in the stern, his head on the cushion, asleep. They woke him, and said to him, 'Master, do you not care? We are lost!' And he woke up, and rebuked the wind and said to the sea, 'Quiet now! Be calm!' And the wind dropped, and there followed a great calm. Then he said to them, 'Why are you so frightened? Have you still no faith?' They were overcome with awe and said to one another, 'Who can this be? Even the wind and the sea obey him.'

The Gospel of the Lord.

PRAYER OF THE FAITHFUL

Let us make our prayers to God, as we pray at the beginning of our school year.

Look after us, Lord, during this coming year; help us live in this school as a Christian community. **Lord hear us**.

We pray for all who work in our school, for teachers and all its staff; bless them and their families. **Lord hear us**.

We pray for all past pupils, and for those who left last year; we remember especially those who are sick, unemployed or in any sort of trouble. **Lord hear us**.

We pray for people who are new in our school, pupils and teachers; may they be happy here and find friends. **Lord hear us**.

For any belonging to us who have died in the past Summer, give them O Lord, eternal joy. **Lord hear us**.

Let us pray.

Help us, Lord, to use well the talents you have given each of us. Help us bring them to our studies so that we work to the best of our ability. May all in this school feel valued, for who we are in your sight. May all we do and learn be in your service, and in the service of love, both now and in the future.

We ask this in the name of Jesus our Lord. Amen.

PRAYER OVER THE GIFTS

Lord God, accept our gifts and see the goodness of your people who offer them to you. Free us from the influence of evil in our lives by the power of Jesus who is Lord for ever. Amen.

REFLECTION

What will this year bring?
We do not know;
It will bring its usual times of work and play,
experiences of success and failure,
all the things that are part of school life.
It is a new beginning;
the planting of a seed that will grow for a year,
the seed of fruit that will blossom in times to come.
It is a new hope;
hope for good work, for successful results,
for friendship, for fun, for learning.
In this coming year, may there be learning, prayer and fun.
May there be hard work, faith and friendship.
May no one in this school be lonely;
may no one be left out in class;
may no one suffer through the others here.
As we begin this year in hope, in prayer and in friendship,
may the Lord begin it with us, be with us during it,
and successfully bring it to its conclusion.

or

Beginning times are times of hope.

We look ahead and hope for the best of times this coming year.

For friendship, learning and enjoyment.

Every beginning is a time of looking forward to doing our best and bringing the best out of each other.

May the goodness of this school inspire us all to making this year good for everyone here.

CONCLUDING PRAYER

May we spread the love, kindness and compassion of God in our school and wherever we are during this coming year. We make this prayer through Christ our Lord. Amen.

2. NOVEMBER MEMORIAL

This was used as an annual memorial for deceased students and staff members in school. It may be adapted for a school community to remember all those who have died in the last year.

PREPARATION

Students may prepare a sacred space in the school with names of those whom they would like to remember during the month of November, and especially today. These names could be displayed on a wall, on the branch of a tree, on stones or in a book. At a funeral you might hear the words 'In baptism you called them to eternal life'. Students could explore the significance of their name and how the act of using another's name calls them into mind and heart. This would also bring more meaning to the reading of the names of the deceased during the liturgy.

INTRODUCTION

There are many different things we can use these days to help us remember things: our phones, sticky notes, a calendar. Sometimes our phones might have an alarm that calls our messages to our attention. In our parish when church bells ring they ring to help us to remember when to pray, when to come and celebrate or when to acknowledge the death of a member of the community. Calling out the name of a deceased loved one in this liturgy similarly helps us call our minds and hearts to those people we remember. We call their names out loud because they are still part of us. And we believe that though their life has changed, it hasn't ended. In our gospel reading, we will see how Mary Magdalene did not recognise the risen Jesus until he called her name.

PENITENTIAL RITE

We come to God, knowing we need his mercy and forgiveness, and we call to mind our sins.

You come to bring us life to the full. **Lord have mercy**.
You are the word of life and bread of life. **Christ have mercy**.
You will come in glory with salvation for us all. **Lord have mercy**.

OPENING PRAYER

We have come together today to remember those from our school community who have died. We remember them with love; glad that they touched our lives and sad that they are no longer with us. We remember them too with the hope that the Lord our God has welcomed them home, and that one day we will be united together in heaven. We ask this through Christ our Lord. Amen.

FIRST READING

Isaiah 49:13-16

God has our name carved in the palm of his hand. We remember those we love who have died and we trust that they are with the risen Jesus.

A reading from the prophet Isaiah.

Shout for joy, you heavens; earth, exult! Mountains, break into joyful cries! They were saying, 'the Lord has abandoned me, the Lord has forgotten me.' Can a woman forget her baby at the breast, feel no pity for the child she has borne? Even if these were to forget, I shall not forget you. Look, I have engraved you on the palms of my hands. I have called you by your name, have given you a title though you do not know me.

The word of the Lord.

RESPONSORIAL PSALM

Psalm 24

The Lord promises heaven to the thief.

Response: This day you will be with me in paradise.

Lord, make your ways known to me,
teach me your paths.
Set me in the way of your truth, and teach me,
for you are the God who saves me. **R**.
All day long I hope in you

because of your goodness, O Lord.
Remember your kindness, Lord,
you love, which you showed long ago.
Do not remember the sins of my youth,
but rather, with your love remember me. **R.**

GOSPEL READING

John: 20:1-2, 11-18

Mary Magdalene didn't recognise Jesus until he called her name. When we look for someone we call them by their name in the hope that it will bring them to us. It brought Mary to the risen Jesus. When we call God's name it brings him closer. Mary was shocked, upset and afraid when she discovered the empty tomb. When Jesus called her name she became the first to spread the good news of his resurrection.

A reading from the holy Gospel according to John.

It was very early on the first day of the week and still dark, when Mary of Magdala came to the tomb. She saw that the stone had been moved away from the tomb and came running to Simon Peter and the other disciple, the one whom Jesus loved. 'They have taken the Lord out of the tomb,' she said, 'and we don't know where they have put him.' But Mary was standing outside near the tomb, weeping. Then, as she wept, she stooped to look inside, and saw two angels in white sitting where the body of Jesus had been, one at the head, the other at the feet. They said, 'Woman, why are you weeping?' 'They have taken my Lord away,' she replied, 'and I don't know where they have put him.' As she said this she turned round and saw Jesus standing there, though she did not realise that it was Jesus. Jesus said to her, 'Woman, why are you weeping? Who are you looking for?' Supposing him to be the gardener, she said, 'Sir, if you have taken him away, tell me where you have put him, and I will go and remove him.' Jesus said, 'Mary!' She turned round then and said to him in Hebrew, 'Rabbuni!' – which means Master. So Mary of Magdala told the disciples, 'I have seen the Lord,' and that he had said these things to her.

The Gospel of the Lord.

REMEMBERING THEM

I have called you by your name and you are mine.
Our name the first gift that we are given.
It identifies us. It is who we are.
When a name is called it invites a response.
There is a relationship involved.
Today we call the names of our loved ones who were present in our lives as members of our family, as friends, classmates, as teachers or colleagues.
When we call their names we remember them and we invite them to remember us. Remember us as a community of mothers, fathers, brothers, sisters, colleagues, teachers, friends, in faith.
Remember us as we remember you.
I have engraved you on the palm of my hand,
your name is engraved deep within our hearts;
I have called you by your name and you are mine,
you have called me by my name and I am yours.

GESTURE

Read slowly the names of those being remembered. As each name is read out a student lights a candle and places it in the sacred space.

or

If there is a smaller group, after the names are read, each person could light a candle in silence or as an appropriate hymn/song is sung for those they are remembering.

PRAYER OF THE FAITHFUL

We pray for all those we remember today and for those whose names are placed in our book of remembrance/ display/ wall/ tree. May they rest in peace and rise in glory.

We pray for those who are mourning their loved ones. Lord carry them lovingly in the palm of your hand. **Lord hear us**.

We pray for the lonely, the weak and the sick that they can find hope and courage from your spirit. **Lord hear us**.

We pray for all who help those who are grieving, may they be blessed with strength and gentleness. **Lord hear us**.

We pray for ourselves that we may touch the lives of others and be a message of hope in times of sadness and confusion. **Lord hear us**.

Let us pray.

Lord God,
May we be strengthened in our loss,
may we be encouraged in the darkness of death
and live our lives in service of you
as we hope to share in the risen life of Christ.
We make our prayer through Christ our Lord. Amen.

PRAYER OVER THE GIFTS

Lord God, Father of our Lord and Brother, Jesus Christ,
we give to you in bread and wine
our sadness and our thanks as we remember our loved ones.
May we all grow in hope this day
as we pray with all who have gone before us,
We ask this in the name of Jesus the Lord. Amen.

REFLECTION

We find ourselves now in your presence, Lord
in the company of all the saints
and in the presence of those we are remembering today.
Family members, friends, classmates, gone before us through death.
Remembered always by us:
laughs, hurts, achievements and failures, friendship and love.
As we remember, help us to find consolation in the good memories we have,
forgiveness for the hurts and hope in the love that never dies.

or

We find ourselves now in your presence Lord,
in the company of all the saints and in the presence of those we are remembering today.
Family members, friends, classmates, gone before us, through death.
Remembered always by us;

laughs, hurts, achievements and failures, friendship and love.
As we remember, help us to find consolation in the good memories we have, forgiveness for the hurts and hope in the love that never dies.

or

In the Eucharist, bread is taken, blessed, broken and given.
In life we are taken, blessed, broken and given.
The priest takes the bread in his hands and blesses it during the Eucharistic prayer,
then he breaks it and it is given to us as the Body of Christ.
Through our birth and baptism we are taken into God's hands, as the bread is taken, so too are we.
In life we are blessed by family, friends, love and joy, as the bread is blessed, so too are we.
We are broken by failure, sin, pain and heartbreak; as the bread is broken, so too are we.
In death we are given back to the mystery from which we came; as the bread is given, so too are we.
When we take, bless, break and give bread to one another, we believe the Lord to be especially present in our midst.
But we must learn to accept that, in his memory, we will be taken, blessed, broken and given for the life of the world.

(Michael Drumm and Tom Gunning)

CONCLUDING PRAYER

Lord, we thank you for this time we have shared today to remember our loved ones. We thank you for the gift of their lives and we place them safely in your care. We pray that they are at peace and we ask for the same peace in our own hearts.

We ask this through Christ our Lord. Amen.

3. DEATH OF A YOUNG PERSON

PREPARATION

These notes may be of help in any school preparation for a funeral Mass or service, noting that the funeral Mass will be in the care of the family and the parish. They may be of help in any school prayer before the funeral or for a Mass later in the school.

INTRODUCTION

Death is always a shock, even more so when it is the death of a young person, known to us for either a short or long time. We have many words and few words: many words to say what's unimportant and few words to say the real, caring things we'd like to say to each other. We come here to remember a young person, to give thanks, even in our grief, for (name) life, to offer each other, and especially those who will most miss them, the consolation of our love and presence; and to offer also the promise of eternal life. Our consolations will be the joyful memories we have; our sadness is that a young person has gone from us, at an age we did not expect. Our sure hope is that the Lord our God will welcome (name) home, and that one day we will be united together in heaven.

or

I welcome you, our friends to (school) to pray for (name) who has passed away. Death has come as another season, an unexpected part of the sequence of life. Sadly instead of light, there is darkness and pain. (This unexpected death is hard for us to take.) But the light comes from our trust in God, our eternal light. Let us take this time of gathering together, of community, of quiet sincerity and of stillness and prayer, to support each other at this sad time. So this morning, as we enter school, the memories of our loved ones are in our minds.

PENITENTIAL RITE

You are the resurrection and the life. **Lord have mercy**.

You raise the dead to life in eternity. **Christ have mercy**.

You will come in glory with salvation for your people. **Lord have mercy**.

OPENING PRAYER

Let us pray.

Lord God, this day we remember all of our family and community who have gone before us, our loved ones, and we entrust them to your living mercy. We pray especially for (name); give us at this sad time faith in your care, hope in your promises and love always. We ask this through Christ our Lord. Amen.

FIRST READING

1 Corinthians 2:3-5

Be encouraged in hard times.

A reading from the second letter of St Paul to the Corinthians.

Grace to you and peace from God our Father and the Lord Jesus Christ. Blessed be the God and Father of our Lord Jesus Christ, the merciful Father and the God who gives every possible encouragement; he supports us in every hardship, so that we are able to come to the support of others in every hardship of theirs because of the encouragement that we ourselves receive from God. For just as the sufferings of Christ overflow into our lives; so too does the encouragement we receive through Christ.

The word of the Lord.

RESPONSORIAL PSALM

Psalm 103

A poem about the love of God.

Response: the Lord is compassion and love.

The Lord has compassion for his people.
The Lord is compassionate and gracious,
slow to anger and rich in mercy.
He will not always find fault;
nor persist in his anger forever. **R.**
For as the heavens are high above the earth,
so strong his mercy for those who fear him.
As far as the east is from the west,
so far from us does he remove our transgressions. **R.**

GOSPEL READING

Luke 10:20-22

Our names are written in heaven.

A reading from the holy Gospel of Luke.

Rejoice that your names are written in heaven. Filled with joy by the Holy Spirit, he said, 'I bless you, Father, Lord of heaven and of earth, for hiding these things from the learned and the clever and revealing them to little children. Yes, Father, for that is what it has pleased you to do. Everything has been entrusted to me by my Father; and no one knows who the Son is except the Father, and who the Father is except the Son and those to whom the Son chooses to reveal him.'

The Gospel of the Lord.

PRAYER OF THE FAITHFUL

We offer prayers to God, the source of all life and love, turning to him for support when death comes.

We pray, in thanks, for (name) and for his / her contribution to our school. We remember (some aspects of his / her life). We pray in thanks for the friendships (name) formed. May his / her spirit continue to inspire us to be the best that we can be. **Lord hear us.**

We pray for (name) family, their parents (name), their brothers (name) and sisters (name). May the Lord guide them as they live their lives with the shock of the loss of (name). May they always find the grace of the Lord in their lives. **Lord hear us.**

We pray for the community of (school), the board, the staff, the students and the parents and past pupils; that we may continue to be a source of respect, friendship and care and continue to be a welcoming place for those who have been part of our community. **Lord hear us.**

We ask the Lord to guide us, as we reach out to our friends. **Lord hear us.**

We pray for those whom we have known and loved and are now in the hands of the Lord. We pray for young and old, those who have had an untimely or sudden passing and those who suffered in sickness. Especially today we remember those who are part of our school's list of the deceased. May they rest in peace. **Lord hear us.**

We pray that our faith may endure through the dark times especially through the pain of tragic loss. May we trust in you now and always. **Lord hear us**.

We pray for the friends and families gathered here today. May the Lord guide you as you live your life with the loss of your loved ones. May you always find the grace of the Lord through your prayers. **Lord hear us**.

As young people, we pray in a special way for all parents who grieve over the death of their children. May they may be comforted in the knowledge that their precious sons and daughters rest in God. **Lord hear us**.

Let us pray.

Hear O Lord our prayers on this sad day. Give us all patience in accepting our loss, and console us with the friendship of each other and our love. We ask this through Christ our Lord. Amen.

PRAYER OVER THE GIFTS

Let us pray.

We offer you this day O Lord, the bread and wine you have created for our nourishment. May your peace and kindness be with us this day. We ask this through Christ our Lord. Amen.

REFLECTION

The reassuring words of the prayer of St Francis of Assisi.

Lord, make me an instrument ofYour Peace;
Where there is hatred, let me sow Love;
Where there is injury, pardon;
Where there is doubt, faith;
Where there is despair, hope;
Where there is darkness, light;
Where there is sadness, joy.
O Divine Master, grant that I may seek
not so much to be consoled, as to console;
to be understood as to understand;

to be loved as to love;
for it is in giving that we receive;
it is in pardoning that we are pardoned;
and it is in dying that we are born to Eternal Life. Amen.

or

In the rising of the sun and its going down,
we will remember (name).
In the blowing of the wind and in the chill of winter,
we will remember (name).
In the opening of buds and in the rebirth of spring,
we will remember (name).
In the blueness of the sky and in the warmth of summer,
we will remember (name).
In the rustling of leaves and in the beauty of autumn,
we will remember (name).
In the beginning of the year and when it ends,
we will remember (name).
When we are weary and in need of strength
we will remember (name).
When we are lost and sick at heart,
we will remember (name).
When we have joys and special celebrations we wish to share,
we will remember (name).
So long as we live, (name) too shall live, for (name) is part of us,
we will remember (name).

(Old Jewish Prayer)

CONCLUDING PRAYER

Let us pray.
Bless all of us who pray for (name) this day O Lord; welcome home (name) whom we miss so much. Comfort and console their family and friends. May we all find faith in your promise of care in all our days. We make our prayer through Christ our Lord. Amen.

4. GRADUATION

PREPARATION

Get sixth years to reflect on the blessings they have received during their time in school and to symbolise that in ways they choose.

or

Use symbols of the class as a whole, and of their relationship with the school. The following might be used as class symbols.

A school or class mascot: a reminder of our beginning here at (school) when we were invited to take our mascot on our adventure for the next six years.

A statue of people holding hands: a reminder of the bonds that have been made between students and staff.

A friendship bracelet: representing the friendships that we have made and the hope we have to stay in contact with our classmates.

The school journal: representing the life and image we display through our school, our school rules and our motto.

Sports trophies: a reminder of the dedication and talent our year has shown in sport here in school.

A programme from a school musical: a reminder of the musical and theatrical talent present in our school.

Two school roll books (one from first year, and one from sixth year): this stands for all the students that have been part of our year from beginning to end, as each has contributed their own unique qualities to make our stay here so memorable.

INTRODUCTION

We're here today to remember, to pray and to think in hope about the future. We thank God for our times together, for the friends we made, for all we've learnt about life from teachers and from each other. We're here too so that we can pray for each other, for the happiness of each of us in the future. This is a time of some sadness and some joy – sad to leave a lot behind, but joy in moving on. We pray also for ourselves in the coming exams, for peace of mind and for success in them. We look ahead in hope and know that God will be with us in the future as he has been with us up to now. With a sense of joy and of thanks, we now begin our prayer.

PENITENTIAL RITE

For times when we get carried away and are unfair to people. **Lord have mercy**.
For times when we let anger get the better of us. **Christ have mercy**.
For times when we failed to respect ourselves and others around us. **Lord have mercy**.

OPENING PRAYER

Let us pray.

Father, you have filled the hearts of your people with faith, hope and love.
Hear the prayers we offer for the class of 20__.
Give them health in mind and body.
Bless the work that they have done and will do in the coming weeks.
We ask this through our Lord Jesus Christ, your Son,
who lives and reigns with you and the Holy Spirit. Amen.

FIRST READING

Ecclesiastes 3:1-8

A reading from the book of the Ecclesiastes.

Everything happens for a purpose.
There is a season for everything, a time for every occupation under heaven:
A time for giving birth, a time for dying; a time for planting, a time for uprooting what has been planted.
A time for killing, a time for healing; a time for knocking down, a time for building.
A time for tears, a time for laughter; a time for mourning, a time for dancing.

A time for throwing stones away, a time for gathering them; a time for embracing, a time to refrain from embracing.

A time for searching, a time for losing; a time for keeping, a time for discarding.

A time for tearing, a time for sewing; a time for keeping silent, a time for speaking.

A time for loving, a time for hating; a time for war, a time for peace.

The word of the Lord.

RESPONSORIAL PSALM

Psalm 27

Response: the Lord is with us all the days of our life.

The Lord is my light and my shield
whom shall I fear?
The Lord is the stronghold of my life
against whom shall I be afraid? **R.**
I believe I shall see the Lord's goodness
in the land of the living.
Hope in him, hold firm and take heart,
Hope in the Lord. **R.**

GOSPEL READING

Matthew 28:16-20

Jesus' promise to be with us always. This is the promise he mnade to each of us in baptism.

Meanwhile the eleven disciples set out for Galilee, to the mountain where Jesus had arranged to meet them. When they saw him they fell down before him, though some hesitated. Jesus came up and spoke to them. He said, 'All authority in heaven and on earth has been given to me. Go, therefore, make disciples of all nations; baptise them in the name of the Father and of the Son and of the Holy Spirit, and teach them to observe all the commands I gave you. And look, I am with you always; yes, to the end of time.'

The Gospel of the Lord.

PRAYER OF THE FAITHFUL

We pray for the class of 20__ that they have a new beginning in life with peace, happiness, success and love.

We pray for these Leaving Cert students, and the Junior Cert students too: that they achieve great things, and work to the best of their ability. **Lord hear us**.

We pray for and thank God for all the staff who helped us to get through our school years. May they have good health to continue their work and may they have support from everyone to do so. **Lord hear us**.

We pray for all our dead, especially those of our class who died during their time here, may they always be remembered. **Lord hear us**.

We pray for our parents, we thank them for their help and the support that they have given us throughout our time here. May they continue to guide us as we finish school and go out into the world. **Lord hear us**.

Let us pray.

These are our prayers Lord, spoken in your presence.
Hear the unspoken prayers of our hearts
we ask you Lord to guide us through our concerns
so that we may know the comfort of your love.
We ask these prayers through Christ our Lord. Amen.

PRAYER OVER THE GIFTS

Let us pray.
Lord God, may our prayer together
increase our faith in your companionship,
our hope in your love,
our love for your people.
As we offer this bread and wine,
may we be strengthened in our friendship with you,
now and forever.
We ask this through Jesus the Lord. Amen.

REFLECTION

May I become at all times, both now and forever
a protector for those without protection,
a guide for those who have lost their way,
a ship for those with oceans to cross,
a bridge for those with rivers to cross,
a sanctuary for those in danger,
a lamp for those without light,
a place of refuge for those who lack shelter,
and a servant to all in need.

(Dalai Lama)

or

Our lives are marked forever
by those we meet;
the friendships we make and the love we experience,
the reconciliations and the quarrels,
the works we have tried to do together,
for each other and for those less fortunate.
All this has given us something that will last.
Long after we've forgotten the marks of our exams,
we'll remember the friendships, the times of growth,
the fun, the laughter, the jokes.
We'll remember how we helped each other to grow as men and women,
in faith, in hope and in love.
May what we have done in this place
be given to many others in our lives.

CONCLUDING PRAYER

Lord, may your truth and love continue to grow in the hearts of all gathered here.
Bless and guide the class of 20__ in the years ahead,
give them health of mind, soul and body.
Be with those they love now and always.
Grant this through Christ our Lord. Amen.

5. REACHING OUT
FOR BEGINNINGS, ENDINGS, VOLUNTEERING

PREPARATION

This liturgy can be used at the beginning of the year, or to celebrate school spirit or for a sending off of a group of students who are about to partake in volunteer work. If used for the beginning of the year, a commissioning of prefects can be included. It may also serve for use as a commissioning of volunteers. To prepare the sacred space, students can trace their hand on paper and cut it out and write their name and a gift that they have that they can use to help others. These can be displayed then in an open treasure-like chest (with the hands overflowing out of the top) in the centre of the sacred space or simply on posters and hung on the surrounding walls. Other things that could be part of the sacred space are a globe, arrows pointing outwards, pictures of inspirational people who have made a difference by reaching out to others. During this activity the students can be encouraged to talk about how they could reach out and make a difference to someone in need.

INTRODUCTION

We reach out to many people in our lives: looking for help, for a listening ear, for advice. We also reach out to give what we can of our talents and our abilities. The Christian reaches out in love, and we offer love we are offering something of ourselves and God's gift to each other. Each of us treasured in love by others and by God. The personality of each person enriches the life of our class and our school.

PENITENTIAL RITE

You reach out to us in love. **Lord have mercy**.
You reach out to us with justice for your people. **Christ have mercy**.
You reach out to us with friendship forever. **Lord have mercy**.

OPENING PRAYER

As I stand before you Lord with my arms open wide, reaching out, I can only reach so far. When all of us together reach out, we can go so much further. Open our arms and our hearts Lord this year and help us to reach out to make this beautiful world you have given us even better. We ask this through Christ our Lord. Amen.

FIRST READING

1 Corinthians 12:31-13:8

A well known piece from St Paul on the qualities of reaching out to people.

A reading from the first letter of St Paul to the Corinthians.

Set your mind on the higher gifts. And now I am going to put before you the best way of all. Though I command languages both human and angelic – if I speak without love, I am no more than a gong booming or a cymbal clashing. And though I have the power of prophecy, to penetrate all mysteries and knowledge, and though I have all the faith necessary to move mountains – if I am without love, I am nothing. Though I should give away to the poor all that I possess, and even give up my body to be burned – if I am without love, it will do me no good whatever. Love is always patient and kind; love is never jealous; love is not boastful or conceited, it is never rude and never seeks its own advantage, it does not take offence or store up grievances. Love does not rejoice at wrongdoing, but finds its joy in the truth. It is always ready to make allowances, to trust, to hope and to endure whatever comes. Love never comes to an end.

The word of the Lord.

RESPONSORIAL PSALM

Psalm 139

Response: the Lord reaches out to us in love.

For it was you who formed my inmost being,
knit me together in my mother's womb.
I thank you who wonderfully made me;
how wonderful are your works,

which my soul knows well! **R.**
My frame was not hidden from you,
when I was being fashioned in secret
and molded in the depths of the earth. **R.**

GOSPEL READING

Matthew 6:19-21

One of our biggest reassures is our ability and dream to reach out to others in love.

Do not store up treasures for yourselves on earth, where moth and woodworm destroy them. But store up treasures for yourselves in heaven, where neither moth nor woodworm destroys them and thieves cannot break in and steal. For wherever your treasure is, there will your heart be too.

COMMISSIONING OF PREFECTS

Priest/Leader: you are asked to serve as student leaders of this community. To use the gifts you have to make a difference. We pray for you to be blessed and supported by God and by this school community. Do you commit yourselves to the role?

Prefects: I do.

Priest/Leader: will you speak openly with honesty and courage, listen patiently with kindness and show leadership in your thoughts and actions? Will you look out for the vulnerable and be inclusive in your work?

Prefects: I will.

Priest/Leader: will you work as a team with one another and with the rest of the community of this school towards making your school a safe, warm and caring place where we are committed to striving for excellence and the growth of each student to their full potential?

Prefects: we will.

Priest/Leader: may you always use wisely the gifts you have and we pray too that you can use the graces that you don't know you have. We make this prayer through Christ our Lord.

All: Amen.

Blessing: *all say*. May we be blessed in our leadership role in our school. May we be people of responsibility, joy and encouragement to all. May we bring the blessing of God to all we meet this year. Amen.

PRAYER OF THE FAITHFUL

We pray for the gift of respect, that we may respect the earth, all its plants and animals, that we can respect one another and most of all that we may respect ourselves.

We pray for peace. We remember especially the people in our world who need peace most, the people of (name of places in most need of peace) and people in our own country whose lives are troubled. Help us be peacemakers and bring comfort to the suffering. **Lord hear us**.

We pray for the gift of love. May we be able to show our good heart, by being caring, by including everyone, by sharing our time, especially with the elderly, may we also know that we are loved, by our families, and friends and by God our Father. **Lord hear us**.

We pray that we may be able to delight in the good, that we can recognise all the good things that surround us and be grateful for them, no matter how small, and be especially grateful for the talents we have that we can share. **Lord hear us**.

We pray for the gift of forgiveness, that we may be able to forgive others and ourselves; and that we may be freed of any grudges that put us in bad moods. **Lord hear us**.

We pray for a new start. May we at the beginning of this year make a new start and endeavour to live our lives to the fullest of our potential so that we can always try and do our best. **Lord hear us**.

Let us pray.

Hear our prayers O Lord which we make to you as our way of reaching out to many others, as you did in the life of your Son. Amen.

PROCESSION AND OFFERING

Note: As some of the gifts to offer cannot be physically seen, a poster with the word in large print, or a clear illustration of the gift is carried forward and placed in the sacred space or in front of the altar.

Student: For our offertory procession, the gifts that we bring up are the gifts that we hope to share this year in (name of school).

Sixth year brings up: leadership.

Fifth Year brings up: talents.

Fourth Year brings up: community.

Third Year brings up: charity.

Second Year brings up: friendship.

First Year brings up: learning.

PRAYER OVER GIFTS

Take these gifts O Lord of bread and wine and change them we pray into the Body and Blood of your Son, Christ our Lord. Amen.

REFLECTION

Prayer of St Theresa of Ávila.

Christ has no body now on earth but yours,
no hands but yours,
no feet but yours,
yours are the eyes through which to look out
Christ's compassion to the world.
Yours are the feet with which he is to go about
doing good;
yours are the hands with which he is to bless others now.

CONCLUDING PRAYER

Let us pray.

Be with us Lord in all we do or say; may our words and action reach out to others in love as your Son Jesus always did. We make this prayer in his name, Christ our Lord. Amen.

6. DECEMBER 8TH
FEAST OF THE IMMACULATE CONCEPTION

This can be used and adapted for other Marian feasts.

PREPARATION

Senior students could prepare for this feast day by looking at the religious meaning of the word grace and/or taking a look at the Magnificat or the Hail Mary to see how Mary is presented to us in the Bible and in our faith. Junior students could prepare by making posters in different languages and placing them in the sacred space or around the school saying 'God loves you!'

INTRODUCTION

Today is the feast of Mary becoming full of grace from the moment she was conceived – the Immaculate Conception. This was the gift she was given – to know, as she grew, how much she was loved by God. She lived her life out of that love. I wonder if we knew how much we are loved by God would it change the way we live our lives? God was there for her when she needed God. As she grew her life became extraordinary, something in Mary was awoken, and she was the first to know that God was with us – Immanuel. She gave birth to God's own son. And God was always with her, through Jesus' childhood, ministry, death on a cross and his resurrection. Mary witnessed this – knowing and believing through it all that God's love for her was greater than she could imagine – she was full of grace.

or

Today we remember Mary, mother of God, and a sort of mother to the apostles. At this time (month of May…special feast…commemoration of mothers), we remember her as the woman of faith and love. Her faith was ordinary at times, and very tested. Her strength was from the love she knew from and with her son. She has been a significant helper to us over the years and we ask her help in our prayer today.

PENITENTIAL RITE

Lord Jesus, you are Son of God and Son of Mary. **Lord have mercy**.
Lord Jesus, you have come to save sinners. **Christ have mercy**.
Lord Jesus, you plead for us with our Father in heaven. **Lord have mercy**.

OPENING PRAYER

Pour forth we ask you, O Lord, your grace into our hearts, that we to whom the incarnation of Christ your Son was made known by the message of an angel, may by his passion and cross be brought to the glory of his resurrection, through Christ our Lord. Amen.

FIRST READING

Isaiah 9:1,5-7

Because of the response of Mary to God, the light of God, Jesus Christ entered into the world. This passage of the bible was one Mary would have read many times herself, as she pondered on her own calling by God – the promise of God to send Christ into the world.

The people that walked in darkness
have seen a great light.
On those who live in a land of deep shadow
a light has shone.
You have made their gladness greater,
you have made their joy increase.
For there is a child born for us
a son given to us
and dominion is laid on his shoulders;
and this is the name they give him:
Wonder-Counsellor, Mighty-God,
Eternal-Father, Prince of Peace.
Wide is his dominion
in a peace that has no end.
From this time onwards and forever
the love of the Lord God will do this.

The word of the Lord.

RESPONSORIAL PSALM

Modern Magnificat

My soul sings in gratitude.
I'm dancing in the mystery of God.
The light of the Holy One is within me
and I am blessed, so truly blessed.

This goes deeper than human thinking.
I am filled with awe
at Love whose only condition
is to be received.

The gift is not for the proud,
for they have no room for it.
The strong and self-sufficient ones
don't have this awareness.

But those who know their emptiness
can rejoice in Love's fullness.
It's the Love that we are made for,
the reason for our being.
It fills our inmost heart space
and brings to birth in us, the Holy One.

(Joy Cowley)

GOSPEL READING

Luke 1: 26-38

In our Gospel today we hear the story of the announcement the Angel Gabriel made to Mary – that she would have God's son. We hear that she is highly favoured. She knows God loves her. Her relationship with God was one of deep understanding. She says she is God's servant – selfless rather than self-centred.

A reading from the holy Gospel according to Luke.

In the sixth month the angel Gabriel was sent by God to a town in Galilee called Nazareth, to a virgin betrothed to a man named Joseph, of the House of David; and the virgin's name was Mary. He went in and said to her, 'Rejoice, you who enjoy God's favour! The Lord is with you.' She was deeply disturbed by these words and asked herself what this greeting could mean, but the angel said to her, 'Mary, do not be afraid; you have won God's favour. Look! You are to conceive in your womb and bear a son, and you must name him Jesus.He will be great and will be called Son of the Most High. The Lord God will give him the throne of his ancestor David; he will rule over the House of Jacob for ever and his reign will have no end.'

Mary said to the angel, 'But how can this come about, since I have no knowledge of man?'

The angel answered, 'The Holy Spirit will come upon you, and the power of the Most High will cover you with its shadow. And so the child will be holy and will be called Son of God.

And I tell you this too: your cousin Elizabeth also, in her old age, has conceived a son, and she whom people called barren is now in her sixth month, for nothing is impossible to God.'

Mary said, 'You see before you the Lord's servant, let it happen to me as you have said.' And the angel left her. Yes, blessed is she who believed that the promise made her by the Lord would be fulfilled.'

The Gospel of the Lord.

PRAYERS OF THE FAITHFUL

We pray for our leaders, in our school, the Church and all world leaders, may they act with compassion and love for the vulnerable and needy.

We pray that we may follow Mary's example, growing in faith and love, asking for the courage to let God work in our lives. **Lord hear us**.

We pray for those who are poor, those who have addictions, those who have been abused in life, may they find help and your love in the love of others. **Lord hear us**.

We pray for anyone we know who has died. May the Lord welcome them home and comfort those who miss them.

We pray for the graces that we don't know that we need. **Lord hear us**.

Let us pray.

We pray now through Mary's intercession that we may be helped in our lives by her prayer and example; may we be people of faith, hope and love, and may we be strengthened in our lives by the knowledge that always God loves us first. We make this prayer through Christ our Lord. Amen.

OFFERTORY

As this feast takes place during Advent, perhaps something representing such an activity for those in need could be brought forward, offered, on behalf of the school community. For example, a Christmas shoebox, a food hamper, a hat and scarf for the homeless. Remembering that God 'has filled the hungry with rich things'.

PRAYER OVER THE GIFTS

May the bread and wine we offer Lord symbolise the love we give to others in life. May we work with Mary for the improvement of our world. Through Christ our Lord. Amen.

REFLECTION

Full of grace
knowing that you are loved by God,
loved before you were born,
it's a love you don't earn.
You don't have to prove yourself to receive it.
It's totally free.
Knowing you are loved by God in this way is a gift;
accepting this gift is really getting to know God deeply.
You are full of grace,
grace that will help you to do good;
when you feel weak, grace will help you carry on.
Grace that will help you see the needs of others and serve them,
and resist serving only yourself.
Hail Mary, you are full of grace
the Lord is with you,
blessed are you among us

and blessed is the fruit of your womb Jesus.
Help us to be like you and trust how much God loves us
so we can show that love to the world.

or

Mary seems to find God in the ordinary human side of her life.
Because Mary knew weakness she could know God.
She could shout to all that 'God does great things for me'.
If we think we have things all together,
then we find little need for God. God will be missing, and not missed.
Much of the gospel of her Son will be finding and helping people at their worst.
She will often be present at times of people's great needs,
like at the wedding feast of Cana and later at Calvary.
It's the same for ourselves.
We are loved most by God when we are at our weakest.
God loves us most when we love ourselves least.
Thanks be to God.

CONCLUDING PRAYER

Let us pray

Give to us, O Lord, the grace you gave to Mary, our sister and friend in your name and love. Give us the wish to do our best in life always for you and our world. We make this prayer through Christ our Lord. Amen

7. ADVENT

PREPARATION

To help us prepare this celebration, we bring forward our symbols of preparation and place at the foot of our altar.

We bring an empty crib, reminding us of the space we need to prepare for the coming of Jesus into our lives.

We bring candles to light our altar, reminding us that Christ is our light who overcomes all parts of darkness in our lives.

We bring the Bible, where the sacred and holy story of the journey and the preparation for the first Christmas is told.

or

To help us prepare this celebration, we bring forward our symbols that remind us of the importance of Advent as we prepare for Christmas.

We bring our Advent words: love, joy, hope and peace, reminding us of the gifts that Jesus' birth offers us.

We place a Star at the foot of the altar reminding us that we need direction in our life's journey. This direction is found through the gift of faith.

Finally, we bring the Bible. It is opened on the page that tells us the story of Jesus's birth. Jesus' birth is a gift to us from God to be celebrated here and now.

INTRODUCTION

Advent is a time set aside to prepare for the feast of Christmas. We prepare as individuals, as family members and as a community. It can be a fun time as well as a very busy time. However, during this time, it is important to stop and reflect on the meaning of Christmas. Let us now prepare some quiet time to pray for what is important to us as individuals, as family members and as a school community. During this time, we ask God to lead our prayer in this celebration of the Eucharist.

PENITENTIAL RITE

As we call to mind the heart of God and the value of each person, we confess that we have not always treated everyone with dignity, nor with the respect that is their due.

Lord Jesus, you are fullness of life, show us your way. **Lord have mercy**.

Lord Jesus, you come with peace and goodwill for all your people. **Christ have mercy**.

Lord Jesus, you are raised from death at the right hand of God. **Lord have mercy**.

OPENING PRAYER

God our Father, as we draw closer to the feast of Christmas, may we allow Christ's values to be born anew in our hearts. May we recognise our need for the sacred gifts of joy, love, hope and peace in our lives. This we ask through Christ, our Lord. Amen.

FIRST READING

Philippians 4:4-7

A reading from the book of Philippians.

Rejoice in the Lord always. I will say it again: rejoice! Let your gentleness be evident to all. The Lord is near. Do not be anxious about anything, but in everything, by prayer and petition, with thanksgiving, present your requests to God. And the peace of God, which transcends all understanding, will guard your hearts and your minds in Christ Jesus.

The word of the Lord.

RESPONSORIAL PSALM

Psalm 41

The world is longing for God.

Response: my soul is thirsting for the living God: when shall I see him face to face?

Like the deer that yearns
for running streams,
so my soul is yearning

for you, my God. **R.**
O send forth your light and your truth;
let these be my guide.
Let them bring me to your holy mountain
to the place where you dwell. **R.**

GOSPEL READING

Luke 2:1-5

A reading from the holy Gospel according to Luke.

About that time Caesar Augustus ordered a census to be taken throughout the Empire. This was the first census when Quirinius was governor of Syria. Everyone had to travel to his own ancestral hometown to be accounted for. So, Joseph went from the Galilean town of Nazareth up to Bethlehem in Judah, David's town, for the census. As a descendant of David, he had to go there. He went with Mary, his fiancée, who was pregnant. While they were there, the time came for her to give birth. She gave birth to a son, her firstborn. She wrapped him in a blanket and laid him in a manger, because there was no room in the inn.

The Gospel of the Lord.

PRAYER OF THE FAITHFUL

As we prepare for the coming of Jesus during this season of Advent, we now present to God our father, our intentions as a community in waiting.

Response: Jesus, our hope is in you.

As we look forward to the birth of Jesus with Christians all over the world, may it bring about everlasting peace and unity for all people especially in countries ravaged by war. We pray to the Lord. **R.**

For all those in our community and beyond who will not receive much this Christmas. May they be comforted by a stranger's kindness and see Jesus in their lives. We pray to the Lord. Jesus, our hope is in you. **R.**

As we wait for Jesus' birth, may our hearts be prepared as we try to be more gentle, kind, giving, and forgiving to our friends and families. We especially remember all separated from those they love. We pray to the Lord, Jesus, our hope is in you. **R.**

As we prepare for the important occasions that lead us to Christmas, we remember those who will travel short and long distances; may the Lord guide them safely. We pray to the Lord. **R.**

Let us pause to silently pray for any special needs of our own. We pray to the Lord. **R.**

We join these prayers with a prayer to the Mother of Jesus who was the first person to prepare for Jesus entering our human family. We pray Hail Mary…

GIFT BEARERS

Four students carrying bread, wine, water and a chalice.

PRAYER OVER THE GIFTS

God, Father, we bring you the gifts of our human toil. We ask you to humbly accept these gifts. Transform them so that we may grow like you each day. We ask you now to transform us so we can become a more loving people, so that everything we do reflects the presence of Christ within us. We ask this in the name of Jesus the Lord. Amen.

REFLECTION

Nobody thought he'd come like he did:
born like a poor child, in a borrowed house,
the son of a woman seeming no different from any other,
except in her glowing faith and huge generosity.
Long after the kings who envied him have been forgotten,
the name of Jesus, Son of God and Son of Mary,
is remembered in lands not even then heard of.
Long after Mary's own birthplace is forgotten,
or the shape of her face and the age of her death,
we remember that she was a woman who gave to God
her whole life, her whole womanhood,
and because of that 'all generations call her blessed'.
Mary, you remind us of what's best in our human nature –

sympathy, compassion, motherhood, love and care.
You remind us too that we are made not just for this life
because as you are now, we one day shall be
through the grace and gift of God.

CONCLUDING PRAYER

We pray, Lord God, that each person here may experience the gifts of love, joy, hope and peace in their lives. May our time at Christmas be not just for ourselves but all the people we will meet. May we have the strength to bring God's kindness into our world. May the witness of our life, prepare us for the birth of Jesus this Christmas.

We ask this through Christ our Lord. Amen.

8. JANUARY 6TH
FEAST OF THE EPIPHANY

PREPARATION

As we return to school, we conclude the Christmas season by celebrating the feast of the Epiphany. Preparation with students can be difficult as often this feast coincides with the start of the new school term, so this material could be better used in prayer services to be celebrated in class groups over the initial week of school. When schools return, it is important to ensure that the oratory/ prayer space/chapel remains appropriate to the Christmas Season.

Suggestions for sacred space in front of altar: have the Bible open on Matthew 2:1-12, a crib including the wise men, a star and a lighting candle. Another suggestion is to include a 'gift-box wrapped in Christmas paper'. We ask everyone to prepare a prayer on a piece of prayer and insert it into the 'gift-box' as they enter the chapel. This box of prayers will be presented during the service.

PRESENTATION OF GIFTS

Gift of Bread: this food is our the basic diet. May we give thanks for the food we receive each day.

Gift of Water: as people travel, it is important that people drink water and stay hydrated. May we remember that fresh water is gifted to us from God our creator.

Gift of the Map: as people travel, they follow many signposts on their journey. Today we pray that God will be our signpost in life especially in times of difficulty.

INTRODUCTION

We gather today to celebrate the feast of the Epiphany which commemorates the wise men who travelled to greet the baby Jesus in the stable in Bethlehem. The gospel describes these visitors as the Magi, wise men who followed a star across the desert to pay homage to the baby Jesus. The Magi brought three significant gifts: the gifts of Gold, Frankincense and Myrrh.

Gold was a precious and expensive gift: the wise men offered this in acknowledgement that Jesus was a king for all people.

Frankincense was a perfume, used in prayer to God: this gift was offered in recognition that Jesus was the saviour for all people.

Myrrh was an ointment which was used in preparation of the body of the deceased before entering the tomb: offering myrrh was the Magi's way of acknowledging the sacrifice that lay ahead for Jesus in our world.

PENITENTIAL RITE

Let us spend some quiet time, reflecting on Christmas.

For the times, we failed to show love in our families we are sorry. **Lord have mercy**.

For the times, we failed to show gratefulness, we are sorry. **Christ have mercy**.

For the times, we failed to listen to God's message of peace, joy, love and hope, we are sorry. **Lord have mercy**.

OPENING PRAYER

Lord God, on the feast of the Epiphany, we remember the three people who journeyed through dangerous lands risking life to seek and worship Jesus the Saviour. We ask for the courage and strength to live a life like Jesus with our families and in our communities. We make our prayer through Christ our Lord. Amen.

FIRST READING

Isaiah 60:1-3

A reading from the prophet Isaiah.

Jerusalem, stand up! Shine! Your new day is dawning. The glory of the Lord shines brightly on you. The earth and its people are covered with darkness, but the glory of the Lord is shining upon you. Nations and kings will come to the light of your dawning day.

The word of the Lord.

RESPONSORIAL PSALM

Psalm 72

Response: Lord, every nation on earth will adore you.

O God, with your judgment endow the king,
and with your justice, the king's son;
he shall govern your people with justice
and your afflicted ones with judgment. **R.**
For he shall rescue the poor when he cries out,
and the afflicted when he has no one to help him.
He shall have pity for the lowly and the poor;
the lives of the poor he shall save. **R.**

GOSPEL READING

Matthew 2:1-12

Let us listen to the story of how they found the holy family by following a star.

A reading from the holy Gospel according to Matthew.

Jesus was born in the town of Bethlehem in Judea, during the time when Herod was king. Soon afterwards, some men who studied the stars came from the east to Jerusalem and asked, 'Where is the baby born to be the king of the Jews? We saw his star when it came up in the east, and we have come to worship him.' When King Herod heard about this, he was very upset, and so was everyone else in Jerusalem. He called together all the chief priests and the teachers of the Law and asked them, 'Where will the Messiah be born?'

'In the town of Bethlehem in Judea,' they answered. 'For this is what the prophet wrote: "Bethlehem in the land of Judah, you are by no means the least of the leading cities of Judah; for from you will come a leader who will guide my people Israel."' So Herod called the visitors from the east to a secret meeting and found out from them the exact time the star had appeared. Then he sent them to Bethlehem with these instructions: "Go and make a careful search for the child, and when you find him, let me know, so that I too may go and worship him."

And so they left, and on their way they saw the same star they had seen in the east. When they saw it, how happy they were, what joy was theirs! It went ahead of them until it stopped over the place where the child was.

They went into the house, and when they saw the child with his mother Mary, they knelt down and worshipped him. They brought out their gifts of gold, frankincense and myrrh and presented them to him.

Then they returned to their own country by another road, since God had warned them in a dream not to go back to Herod.

The Gospel of the Lord.

PRAYERS OF THE FAITHFUL

Having met Mary, Joseph and the baby Jesus, the wise men returned home. They returned to tell the good news about the new saviour to their families and friends. The story of the birth of Jesus reminds us of the good news that God is always with us. Let us remember this in a very special way today as we begin a new year and a new term together.

Response: Lord hear our prayer.

The Magi showed great courage. They left their home and their families without being sure of the way. Let us pray for those who have embarked on journeys in more recent times; the people who have left their homes because of hunger and war. May God guide them and bring them to a place where they know lasting peace and safe lodgings. We pray to the Lord. **R.**

As we return after our Christmas celebrations, we pray in thanksgiving for all we have received, especially from our families. We ask God to continue to bless our relationships with kindness and joy. We pray to the Lord. **R.**

We remember those for whom Christmas has not been a happy time. For those who are homeless, for those who are suffering bereavement and those who are worried and concerned for whatever reason, we ask God to be with them as we pray to the Lord. **R.**

As we begin this New Year, we ask God to bless our promises and good intentions. May we have the convictions and the courage to show God's love through our daily actions. We pray to the Lord. **R.**

Let us pray:

God of our journeys, we offer you the joys and sorrows of our life. May we share the love of your Son with all those we meet this week. We ask this through Christ our Lord. Amen.

REFLECTION

'The Road Not Taken' by Robert Frost

or

People find God in many different ways, such as: prayer, nature, love, sacraments and even suffering. People also find God through asking questions: about the depths of the meaning of life, and about who God is. Like the Magi, we find God in our own way, each of us following a personal star leading to God. The Magi were people who did not follow a way to God ordinary to their time, yet they found their way nonetheless. All of his life, Jesus, the child of Bethlehem, reached out to everyone, finding them as they looked for him. He found them in religious and non-religious places. The Magi were true to their search and found God in a child.

or

Prayer for Refugees

For all those who see 'home'
and all it means
disappears behind them as they flee;
for all those who cannot see a home
in the days ahead of them;
for all who dwell in daily insecurity
in tents and camps;
For those who are weary and without hope in the days ahead;
For all members of refugee
families we pray.
May the image of the holy family
fleeing oppression
stay with us as we pray
for your displaced children;
during the day,

and each night
as we are blessed
with returning to a home.
May we also be blessed
with compassion for those still weary ,
still uprooted,
still far from home. Amen.

(Education for Justice).

CLOSING PRAYER

Let us pray. Lord our God, we thank you for having come to this earth, born in the simple surroundings of a humble stable. Allow your light to be beacon for all to see, among all who hear your gospel, among all with sincere hearts. May all gathered here become a witness to your life, serving you wherever they go.

We ask this through Jesus Christ, our Lord. Amen.

9. ASH WEDNESDAY

PREPARATION

To prepare the students/staff for receiving ashes, some time could be spent discussing things that can be undertaken or given up that will help a person's heart grow better. Anyone who is receiving ashes could make a private written commitment on a piece of paper, and as they come forward to receive their ashes place their commitment in a basket in the sacred space.

INTRODUCTION

We wear ashes to mark the beginning of Lent, of six weeks of trying to live a good life and get ourselves ready to celebrate the resurrection of Jesus. They are a sign on the outside of what we are doing on the inside – opening our hearts. These ashes will be blessed so that everyone who receives them will share in the blessing of God.

The blessing of ashes replaces the Penitential Rite.

OPENING PRAYER

Father in Heaven,
the light of your truth gives sight to the darkness of sin.
May this season of Lent bring us the blessing
of your forgiveness and the gift of your light.
Grant this through Christ Our Lord. Amen.

FIRST READING

Isaiah 58:6-8

What to do for Lent? Care for the needy should be a result of everything we do.

A reading from the prophet Isaiah.

Is not this the sort of fast that pleases me: to break unjust fetters, to undo the thongs of the yoke, to let the oppressed go free and to break all yokes? Is it not sharing your food with the hungry, and sheltering the homeless poor; if you see someone lacking clothes, to clothe him, and not to turn away from your own kin? Then your light will blaze out like the dawn and your wound be quickly healed over. You will be called 'Breach-mender', 'Restorer of streets to be lived in'.

The word of the Lord.

RESPONSORIAL PSALM

Psalm: 51:1-17

A poem of sorrow for sin.

Response: Have mercy on me, God, in your kindness.

Have mercy on me, God, in your kindness,
in your compassion blot out my offence.
O wash me more and more from my guilt,
and cleanse me from my sin. **R.**
My offences truly I know them,
my sin is always before me.
Against you, you alone, have I sinned
what is evil in your sight I have done. **R.**

GOSPEL READING

Mark 6:1-6;16-21

The message of Lent is to change our lives to be more Christian, more unselfish, more compassionate and kind. This is the beginning of the message of Jesus.

A reading from the holy Gospel according to Mark.

After John had been arrested, Jesus went into Galilee. There he proclaimed the Good News from God. 'The time has come', he said 'and the kingdom of God is close at hand. Repent, and believe the Good News.'

This is the Gospel of the Lord.

BLESSING THE ASHES

Lord, we bless these ashes. Once they were leaves of palm used to honour and praise, now they are bits of dust, so fragile they can be blown away by the wind.

They are reminders that we came from the earth and it is to the earth we will return. They remind us that we are sinners and that we need a change of heart. Bless these ashes and bless those who wear them, create in us a clean heart that can make a difference in the world. In the name of the Father, and of the Son and of the Holy Spirit. Amen.

DISTRIBUTION OF THE ASHES

As ashes are place on foreheads the words*: repent and believe the good news* are said or *remember, you are dust and to dust you will return.* As each person receives ashes they can place their Lenten commitments in a basket/box provided in the sacred space.

PRAYERS OF THE FAITHFUL

We gather our prayers in the name and love of Jesus, our Lord and Brother.

We pray Lord that during this time of Lent we can change our hearts for the better. **Lord hear us**.

We pray for the poor of the world and for all of those who work seeking justice and aid for the poor, may they find strength to pursue dignity and fairness for all. **Lord hear us**.

We pray for those whose hearts need healing, may the seed of hope of a new start grow in their hearts so that they can find peace and joy. **Lord hear us**.

We pray for the leaders of our world, that they can have the courage to make the right decisions for the right reasons. **Lord hear us**.

We pray for the Pope, may he continue to inspire his people to follow in a life of service and love. **Lord hear us**.

PRAYER OVER THE GIFTS

Lord help us to resist the attraction of evil
in the world and in our hearts.
May we give time this Lent to prayer and to good works.
We ask this in the name of Jesus the Lord. Amen.

REFLECTION

A dark cross made of ash.
A sign that we begin again.
A spring clean of our hearts,
so we can live.
By doing the right thing for the right reason,
by standing up for those who are afraid,
by feeding those who are hungry,
by sharing with the poor,
by including those who are lonely,
by tending those who are sick,
by caring for the earth,
by spending time in the quiet of our hearts to realise God's love for us.
Blessed with these ashes.
Blessed with your love.
Ready to share it with the world.

or

Dust to dust and ashes to ashes;
may we remember this day
that we come from God
and will go to God.
Dust to dust and ashes to ashes;
may we remember this day
that we need the Lord's forgiveness.
Dust to flowers and ashes to glory:
may we remember this day
that Jesus died and rose from death.

CONCLUDING PRAYER

Lord we have now begun our Lenten journey with your blessing.
Help us to always try to make the right decisions for the right reasons,
so that others can see your love through us.
Amen.

10. LENT

PREPARATION

The young people may spend some time decorating paper crosses to reflect the burdens they carry, their worries and things they are sorry for saying or doing in the past. They may also use them to write intentions/promises for Lent. They could draw symbols, use cut out pictures or words and their work would remain private to them. They could place their crosses in a basket in the centre space. They might be encouraged to make a difference, do good deeds/random acts of kindness for Lent.

or

Five large stones are placed on the floor and five pieces of purple cloth are used to cover them after each piece relevant to the stone is read.

Narrator: when we carry stones such as these in our lives, the load becomes unmanageable. On our Lenten journey these faults and failings weigh us down. During Lent we could make an effort to lighten the load and move forward. Often in school we complain about other people's unkindness towards us, particularly when we feel we are the subject of the news going around the school and when others gossip about us. During Lent we could all make an effort to turn way from those feelings which the five stones represent: fear, disrespect, selfishness, envy and intolerance.

1. We remove the stone of fear: fear of being alone; fear of not being accepted; fear of the future (cover the stone with purple cloth).
2. We remove the stone of disrespect: disrespect towards our environment; disrespect towards our elders; disrespect towards those we do not like (cover the stone with purple cloth).
3. We remove the stone of selfishness: selfish with our time; selfish with our possessions; selfish with our friends (cover the stone with purple cloth).
4. We remove the stone of envy: envy of other's possessions; envy of

other's achievements; envy of other's abilities (cover the stone with purple cloth).

5. We remove the stone of intolerance: intolerance of our failings; intolerance of other's failings; intolerance of those in need (cover the stone with purple cloth).

Lent encourages us to do something extra But for the next forty days we could all make an effort to remove those things which harden our hearts. We could in turn make an effort to show that God is important in our lives. We should care more for the Earth and avoid buying things we do not need.

You could give up something, change your social media actions, you could take a moment at the beginning or the end of the day to say prayer or reflect. You could put money in a Trocaire box. You could give time to a person who needs you. You could change the way you impact the environment. You could tell those you love that you love them.

INTRODUCTION

Lent begins on Ash Wednesday and continues for the forty days before Easter. In our busy world, Lent provides us with opportunities to think about our faith, pray more deeply, express sorrow for what we have done or failed to do and show kindness to all. Today we think of Jesus being led into the wilderness. He was tempted there to go away from the work God wanted him to do. We ask God for the help to keep doing what we know is right, especially at times when our good intentions may waver.

PENITENTIAL RITE

We remember in Lent that our faults can lead us away from God; we also remember that God is all forgiving and all loving. So we ask this forgiveness now for everyone here:

You were led by the Spirit to the desert. **Lord, have mercy**.

You were tempted to a life of power and honour and wealth. **Christ have mercy**.

You plead with God for us, your people for whom you died. **Lord, have mercy**.

OPENING PRAYER

Lord God,
help us to know what we ought to do in our lives,
to do it with courage and generosity
and always to live in your love.
We ask this through Christ our Lord. Amen.

FIRST READING

Ezekiel 34:11-16

The name Ezekiel means 'God strengthens'.

A reading from the prophet Ezekiel.

For I shall take you from among the nations and gather you back from all the countries, and bring you home to your own country. I shall pour clean water over you and you will be cleansed. I shall give you a new heart, and put a new spirit in you; I shall remove the heart of stone from your bodies and give you a heart of flesh instead. I shall put my spirit in you, and make you keep my laws, and respect and practice my judgments. You will live in the country which I gave your ancestors. You will be my people and I shall be your God.

The word of the Lord.

RESPONSORIAL PSALM

Psalm 27

A poem of trust in God.

Response: the Lord is my light and my help.

The Lord is my light and my help,
whom shall I fear?
The Lord is the stronghold of my life;
before whom shall I shrink? **R.**
I am sure I shall see the Lord's goodness
in the land of the living.
Hope in him, hold firm and take heart,
Hope in the Lord! **R.**

GOSPEL READING

Mark 1:12-15

In the wilderness Jesus was tempted to depart from what he knew was his life's mission. He knew confusion, questioning, and also knew that God was with him in the tough times of his own life.

A reading from the holy Gospel according to Mark.

And at once the Spirit drove him into the desert and he remained there for forty days, and was put to the test by Satan. He was with the wild animals, and the angels looked after him.

The Gospel of the Lord.

PRAYER OF THE FAITHFUL

Let us pause to remember our intentions. We ask the Lord for help to carry our burdens and say sorry for any hurt we have caused.

We ask that we ourselves always know the care of God in the hard times of our lives. **Lord hear us**.

For people we know who are in any sort of trouble, particularly members of our own families. **Lord hear us**.

For young people who are lost, lonely and confused, we pray they find friendship and a sense of direction in their lives. **Lord hear us**.

We pray that our faith may grow strong, and that doubts and difficulties in faith we have may not bring us away from our interest in God. **Lord hear us**.

For all who have died, people we know and those of our family, and all who have no one to remember them. **Lord hear us**.

Let us pray.

God our Father, hear our prayers which we make in faith, in hope and in love, through Jesus Christ our Lord. Amen.

PRAYER OVER THE GIFTS

Lord God, accept our gifts of bread and wine.
As we receive from this table the Eucharist of your Son,
help us always to look to you for love, meaning and hope in our lives.
We ask this through Christ our Lord. Amen.

REFLECTION

What does it mean to be led into the wilderness?
To find yourself without bearings,
without direction,
without food, drink, company?
For many the wilderness is to be without direction.
Not knowing how to find love, meaning, joy in life.
Losing faith, hope, friends, commitment.
This seems to be part of life.
In the wilderness Jesus was tempted
to lose direction and to change his plans.
What are you tempted by in life?
Do you make unhealthy choices?
Do you sometimes say or do the wrong thing?
Do you spend too much time on social media
instead of talking to those around you?
Can you allow yourself to find refreshment,
faith, self-confidence
when you feel lost in the wilderness of aloneness
or of failure or confusion?
Times of quiet reflection will allow you to consider
how you treat yourself and others and make amends.
In your desert wilderness you will know God:
he comes looking for you then.
May you have the courage to be open to being found
by God.
If you trust and hope you will know that you are not lost,
for he is with you.
It's not that he will bring you to his home
but he will make his home in you.

or

Fast from worry; feast on trusting God.
Fast from complaining; feast on appreciation.
Fast from negatives; feast on affirmatives.

Fast from hostility; feast on tenderness.
Fast from unrelenting pressures; feast from unceasing prayer.
Fast from judging others; feast on Christ dwelling in them.
Fast from fear of illness; feast on the healing power of God.
Fast from discontent; feast on gratitude.
Fast from anger; feast on patience.
Fast from pessimism; feast on optimism.
Fast from bitterness; feast on forgiveness.
Fast from self-concern; feast on compassion for others.
Fast from discouragement; feast on hope.
Fast from suspicion; feast on truth.
Fast from lethargy and apathy; feast on enthusiasm.
Fast from facts that depress; feast on truths that uplift.
Fast from gossip; feast on purposeful silence.
Fast from problems that overwhelm; feast on prayer that sustains.
Fast from thoughts that weaken; feast on promises that inspire.
Fast from apparent darkness; feast on the reality of light.

(Mother Teresa)

CONCLUDING PRAYER

Lord God,
you have given us the food of life at this table.
We have left our crosses and burdens behind
on the altar and now move forward.
Help us always know your friendship in our lives.
In times of sorrow, be our strength
and in times of joy, be our companion.
We ask this through Christ our Lord. Amen.

11. EASTER

PREPARATION

Work could be done with the young people on where they find God in the ordinary. Encourage them to keep a daily journal, where they can write about a day or week in their lives and describe where they saw the face of God. What were their experiences, who did they encounter, where did they see good in action, who did they help as they went about their ordinary lives? What do they take for granted everyday? What does it mean to us in our day to believe that God walks among us and each person is made in God's image?

Gather signs of presence of God in the prayer space – images from daily life such as sunrise, food, rainfall, smiling faces, rainbows and stars.could be used to reflect the presence of God in the world. Spring flowers and candles may also be used to symbolise faith, new life and peace associated with Easter.

In preparation for the prayer service, students might research the concept of 'joy'. They might research and create symbols of joy and create a display for the prayer space.

or

A rewarding class activity during the Easter season might be to reflect on the fruits of the Holy Spirit: love, joy, peace, patience, kindness, goodness, faithfulness, gentleness, self-control.

Each student could design a small wallet-sized card to illustrate one of these. During the prayer service, students could exchange their card with one another during the sign of peace.

INTRODUCTION

This final term in school can be very busy. The joy of Easter can almost be overlooked. Somehow the reflection on sin and suffering during Lent comes more easily to many of us than experiencing the joy and redemption of the Easter season. However, in this we are not alone: the disciples, too, had difficulty at first absorbing the fullness of resurrection joy as we will hear in our gospel today. Jesus is not interested in talking about the past. Instead, he is focused on offering peace, healing and love in the present, with an eye to the future.

PENITENTIAL RITE

Let us ask God's forgiveness for times when we have failed to be people of reconciliation and of justice when we could have been otherwise.

Lord Jesus, you said, 'I have come that you may have joy and have it to the full'. **Lord, have mercy**.

Lord Jesus, you said to your apostles, 'I leave you peace, my peace I give you'. **Christ, have mercy**.

Lord Jesus, you are our risen brother, pleading for us at the right hand of the Father. **Lord, have mercy**.

OPENING PRAYER

Almighty God,
may the risen power and love of Jesus Christ
be felt in our lives,
our families, our school and our parishes.
May we know it in our country and in our world.
We ask this through Christ our Lord. Amen.

FIRST READING

Acts 2: 22-28

Peter quotes a joyful poem from the bible.

A reading from the Acts of the Apostles.

Then Peter stood up with the Eleven and addressed the crowd in a loud voice: 'Men of Israel, listen to what I am going to say: Jesus the Nazarene was a man commended to you by God, by the miracles and portents and signs that God worked through him when he was among you, as you all know. You killed him, but God raised him to life, for it was impossible for him to be held in the power of death, as David says of him:

"I saw the Lord before me always,

for with him at my right hand nothing can shake me.
So my heart was glad, and my tongue cried out with joy;
my body too will rest in the hope
that you will not abandon my soul to Hades,
nor allow your Holy One to know corruption.
You have made known the way of life to me,
you will fill me with joy through your presence."'
The word of the Lord.

RESPONSORIAL PSALM

Psalm 46

A poem of triumph of God over evil.

Response: Lord, you are our victory over evil.

God is our shelter, our strength,
ever ready to help in time of trouble,
so we shall not be afraid when the earth gives way,
when mountains tumble into the depths of the sea,
and its waters roar and seethe. **R.**
Come, think of the marvels of the Lord,
the astounding things he has done in the world;
all over the world he puts an end to wars,
he breaks the bow, he snaps the spear.
'Pause a while and know that I am God,
exalted among the nations, exalted over the earth.' **R.**

GOSPEL READING

Luke 24:36-43

The apostles are frightened at first at the appearances of Jesus, but eventually they 'are filled with joy'.

A reading from the holy Gospel according to Luke.

They were still talking about all this when he himself stood among them and said to them, 'Peace be with you!' In a state of alarm and fright, they thought they were seeing a ghost. But he said, 'Why are you so agitated, and why are these doubts rising in your hearts? Look at my hands and feet; yes, it is I indeed. Touch me and see for yourselves; a ghost has no flesh and bones as you can see I have.' And as he said this he showed them his hands and his feet. Their joy was so great that they still could not believe it, and they stood there dumbfounded; so he said to them, 'Have you anything here to eat?' And they offered him a piece of grilled fish, which he ate before their eyes.

The Gospel of the Lord.

PRAYER OF THE FAITHFUL

Jesus prayed for peace after his resurrection, and that his followers would be people of unity and of forgiveness. Let's make our intentions now in his name.

Give us joy, Lord, in knowing that you are always with us, a companion in good times and bad, comfort in our losses. **Lord hear us**.

Give peace to troubled parts of the world, especially nations which suffer starvation and drought. **Lord hear us**.

Give hope to people who are down and troubled, especially young people who fear failure and rejection in their lives. **Lord hear us**.

Give eternal joy to all who have died, especially people in our families and others we know. **Lord hear us**.

We pray for the sick, the forgotten, those with disabilities, the lonely: give them the consolation of your risen power. **Lord hear us**.

Let us pray.

God, creator of everything we love, hear our prayer which we make in trust in you. Give us joy and peace this Easter time. Through Christ our Lord. Amen.

PRAYER OVER THE GIFTS

May these gifts we offer
be signs of our love for you, Lord God, and for each other.
As you change them into the body and blood of Jesus,
change us too that we become people of joy and hope.
Grant this through Christ our Lord. Amen.

REFLECTION

They met Jesus after the resurrection.
Apostles, disciples,
searchers, family and friends,
men and women
who had known him,
close followers or some from a distance.
They had felt let down and disappointed.
They found their hearts were lifted after a short time
and faith came back, was recovered and life would never be the same again.

He found them on the road, found them in locked up rooms,
found them in the garden, at the lakeside,
as always, he found them before they found him.
They saw him just for a while.
They heard him, just for a while.
Always, he vanished from their sight.

And the bread remained.
And the echo of his words.
The bread remains today,
food for the journey,
sacrament of salvation,
broken and blessed for the whole world.
Our joy, our call
to lift the world to our God.
One by one, two by two, they came
back to the only place he now belonged,
the garden tomb.
Or so they thought.
The tomb sealed, the spices gone dry,
the linen cloths in their place.
But they could still smell the perfume
and could see the cloths,
but of him they could see nothing.

Hour by hour that day they would not find him,
but he would find them.
They were hardly searching for him,
except the women,
but he found them.
On the Emmaus road, in a room
in a garden,
just in the ordinary.
That's where he belongs.
And we too.
or
Where is the Lord?
Gone away? His work finished?
How are his followers?
Separating? Their hopes finished?
He is with God.
He is raised to God,
he lives now in the place where he was before time began:
with the Father.
He lives with God and he is found in his people;
to be found among people is to be found with God.
Where do we find the one who is with God?
In Galilee, on the road to Emmaus, at the seaside.
Among people.
Lord, help me to notice you,
follow you, enjoy you, embrace you, in your people.
Risen Lord, raise your people!

CONCLUDING PRAYER

Bless us, Lord,
as we leave the table and the Eucharist of your risen Son.
Help us to recognise you in the ordinary.
May we bring with us the hope, peace and joy
which we find in the resurrection of Jesus
who is Lord, today and forever. Amen.

12. FRIENDSHIP

PREPARATION

Students make a friendship tree. The teacher gets a large branch or makes one by drawing it on a large sheet of paper, cutting it out and backing it on cardboard. Students cut out leaf shapes and lightly shade them in green, each student writes a quality of friendship that they value or admire on their leaf and these are attached to the leaf with string. This is placed in the sacred space in the prayer or classroom.

INTRODUCTION

Friendship is what we all need, long for and hope for. It is what causes the greatest joy in our lives, and can also cause the greatest hurts. In friendship we share secrets with another, develop loyalties that are often intense and make relationships that sometimes last long. It may mean moments of just being together, of shared humour, of discovering the mystery and exciting uniqueness of another person, of getting over hurts and misunderstandings. It is important at all ages; without it life can be lonely, empty, isolated. It's the best gift we can give one to another. It is also how Jesus describes his relationship with each of us. He says, 'I do not call you servants, I call you friends.' It's a way of experiencing what God is like. When we try to be true friends to each other we have some glimpse of what God himself is like. We thank God today for friends, pray for them, and welcome Jesus into our lives as a friend.

PENITENTIAL RITE

We call to mind that we are selfish and sinful and that we need God's forgiveness, the forgiveness of Christ, a friend. We ask for forgiveness especially for ways in which we don't spread friendship.

Lord Jesus, you call us friends. **Lord have mercy**.

Christ our Lord, you are a friend of sinners and of everyone. **Christ have mercy**.

Lord Jesus, you show us God as a friend and a father. **Lord have mercy**.

OPENING PRAYER

God, Father, you are the source of all life, and the source of all love.
You have created and formed each person here with the loving hand of care and the caring heart of friendship.
We ask you now to strengthen our belief
in the value and worth we each have in your sight.
Help us believe that each of us delights you,
each of us worth the death of you Son.
We make our prayer through Christ our Lord. Amen.

FIRST READING

Romans 12:9-18

The ways you can recognise Christian friendship are given here by St Paul. The list is impressive and the ideal is high. This is a beautiful vision of what friendship is in the heart of Christ.

A reading from the letter of St Paul to the Romans.

Do not let your love be a pretence, but sincerely prefer good to evil. Love each other as much as brothers and sisters should, and have a profound respect for each other. Work for the Lord with untiring effort and with great earnestness of spirit. If you have hope, this will make you cheerful. Do not give up if trials come; and keep on praying. If any of the saints are in need you must share with them; and you should make hospitality your special care.

Bless those who persecute you: never curse them, bless them. Rejoice with those who rejoice and be sad with those in sorrow. Treat everyone with equal kindness; never be condescending but make real friends with the poor. Do not allow yourself to become self-satisfied. Never repay evil with evil but let everyone see that you are interested only in the highest ideals. Do all you can to live at peace with everyone.

The word of the Lord.

RESPONSORIAL PSALM

Psalm 91

God's love is forever.

Response: I do not call you servants, I call you friends.

He who dwells in the shelter of the Most High
and abides in the shade of the Almighty
says to the Lord: 'My refuge,
my stronghold, my God in whom I trust!' **R.**
His love he set on me, so I will rescue him;
protect him for he knows my name.
When he calls I shall answer: 'I am with you.'
I will save him in distress and give him glory. **R.**

GOSPEL READING

John 15:12-17

Friendship is how Jesus looks on his relationship with his disciples, and this is how he thinks of each of us too.

A reading from the holy Gospel according to John.

One can have no greater love than to lay down his life for his friends. You are my friends if you do what I command you. I shall not call you servants any more, because a servant does not know his master's business; I call you friends, because I have made known to you everything I have learnt from my Father. What I command you is to love one another.

The Gospel of the Lord.

PRAYER OF THE FAITHFUL

We pray now to God for the gift of friendship. We remember people we'd like to pray for.

Response: Lord in your friendship, hear our prayer.

For our friends, we ask you Lord to bless them, especially any of them who are in trouble. **R.**

We ask that we'll always value the gift of friendship, that we don't do anything by gossip or lies to ruin it for others or for ourselves. **R.**

For those who find it hard to make friends, because of shyness or insecurity or embarrassment, or because of problems at home. Lord make us sensitive to them, and let's offer our friendship to them. **R.**

For friendship between nations, for peace and justice in our own countries, and that developed countries may not abuse the poverty of other nations. **R.**

Let us pray.

God our Father, increase in us the desire to make friends, both to be a friend and to receive friendship. Thank you for this gift, and for giving yourself to us as a friend. We pray through Jesus our Lord. Amen.

PRAYER OVER THE GIFTS

Lord God, friend of your people,
friend of the world, friend of the earth:
be with us as we journey together in life to you.
May this bread and wine
always remind us of your friendship
in Jesus Christ our Lord. Amen.

REFLECTION

We are not meant to be alone. Jesus did not call one disciple, he called many, and they travelled together as friends, helping each other, listening to each other, laughing together and sharing tough times with each other. We too need each other, we reach out to each other, it may even be through snap chat or Facebook, but it's important to know that we are not alone. Our friendship tree reminds us of what is important in friendship, the leaves tells us what we look for in a friend, but it also challenges us to reflect on how we show these qualities to others, what kind of a friend am I?

or

We are all moulded and remoulded by those who have loved us and though that love may pass, we remain, none the less, their work. No love, no friendship can ever cross the path of our destiny without leaving some mark upon it forever.

(Francois Mauriac)

CONCLUDING PRAYER

We thank you for this gift of friendship.
Help us to cherish it and nourish it,
and never demean it for anyone.
Make us true friends
in the name and the spirit of Jesus our Lord. Amen.

13. GRATITUDE

PREPARATION

A few days prior to any service, paper stars may be distributed, and students write what they would like to give thanks for in their lives. The stars can be stuck to a board to create a gratitude wall, which can then be used as a backdrop to the liturgy. Alternatively, thank you cards or letters could be written and decorated for display at the prayer. Symbols of joy and thanks might be displayed at the beginning. The following might be used to represent what we are grateful for.

The gift of bread and water (a loaf of bread and bottle of water): we begin with some of our basic needs. May we be grateful for the fact that we have enough to eat and drink every day. May we be mindful of those whose daily life is a struggle for survival.

The gift of family and friends (a photo frame): help us to be grateful for our family and friends. Good relationships require listening, understanding, forgiving and great patience.

The gift of a home (bar of soap and tube of toothpaste): help us to recognise those things that are truly valuable, a home is more than a house. We pray for love, warmth and gentleness. Give us the courage not to seek money and material possessions as if they were the things that matter most.

The gift of communication (a phone): technology helps use to communicate with others and has helped bring us closer to people all over the world. While we are grateful for the ease with which we can talk to people online let us not to forget to talk to those around us.

The gift of the environment (a plant): may we be grateful for the air we breathe and the beauty of our landscape. Help us to develop in ourselves the quality of gentleness. Make us gentle in all our relationships with other people and with the environment.

The gift of our faith (a candle): our faith has been handed down to us from past generations, may we be thankful and carry on the light of faith.

INTRODUCTION

There's a lot in life to be thankful for: friends, family, faith, love, health, talents of the mind, compassion in the heart. We can be thankful for a purpose in our lives, for a job, for enough money to live on; for all the people in our lives, young and old. None of us has everything we want in life, but we can be grateful for all we have. We are grateful for this group here, for the friendship, support, honesty and sincerity among us, and for times we've needed a friend and found one here.

We're grateful also for ways in which we have got strong in difficulties and for our faith in God and his help.

PENITENTIAL RITE

Lord, you have come to bring us joy to the full. **Lord have mercy**.

Lord Jesus, you have come to bring us life to the full. **Christ have mercy**.

Lord, you are the Resurrection and the Life at the right hand of God. **Lord have mercy**.

OPENING PRAYER

Lord God, our life is blessed with many good gifts.
Make us truly grateful
for the gifts of our unique personalities,
for the people who help us in our lives,
and for courage and strength to overcome our difficulties.
We make this prayer though Christ our Lord. Amen.

FIRST READING

Philippians 4:4-20

St Paul is grateful to God for the people he is writing to.

A reading from the letter of St Paul to the Philippians.

I thank my God whenever I think of you and every time I pray for you all, I always pray with joy for your partnership in the gospel from the very first day up to the present.It is only right that I should feel like this towards you all, because you have a place in my heart, since you have all shared together in the grace that has been mine. For God will testify for me how much I long for you all with the warm longing of Christ Jesus; it is my prayer that your love for one another may grow more and more until the Day of Christ comes.

The word of the Lord.

RESPONSORIAL PSALM

Psalm 110

A poem of thanks to God.

Response: We thank the Lord for his goodness to us.

I will thank the Lord with all my heart
in the meeting of the just and their assembly.
Great are the works of the Lord,
to be pondered by all who love them. **R.**
He has sent deliverance to his people
and established his friendship forever.
Holy is his name, to be feared. **R.**

GOSPEL READING

Luke 19:32-41

People praising Jesus as he entered Jerusalem.

A reading from the holy Gospel according to Luke.

So those who were sent departed and found it as he had told them. As they were untying the colt, its owners asked them, 'Why are you untying the colt?' They said, 'The Lord needs it.' Then they brought it to Jesus; and after throwing their cloaks on the colt, they set Jesus on it. As he rode along, people kept spreading their cloaks on the road. As he was now approaching the path down from the Mount of Olives, the whole multitude of the disciples began to praise God joyfully with a loud voice for all the deeds of power that they had seen, saying,

'Blessed is the king
who comes in the name of the Lord!
Peace in heaven,
and glory in the highest heaven!'

Some of the Pharisees in the crowd said to him, 'Teacher, order your disciples to stop.' He answered, 'I tell you, if these were silent, the stones would shout out.'

The Gospel of the Lord.

PRAYERS OF THE FAITHFUL

Let's pray that we may be truly grateful for the gift of God in our lives and that he may work through us for the good of others.

May the Lord bless all those for whom we are grateful, our families, our friends and those who have helped us in any way on our journey of life so far. **Lord hear us**.

May the Lord give us hope and optimism in life, and give us a sense of looking on the good side of things. **Lord hear u**s.

We give thanks for the gift of friendship, we pray we will always value it and treat our friends as we would like to be treated. **Lord hear us**.

We pray for people, especially young people, who find it hard to be grateful, who are depressed and despairing; may they find hope and the friendship of God in their sadness. **Lord hear us**.

We pray for those people in our families and among our friends who have died; may we be truly grateful for them even in the times of loss and mourning. **Lord hear u**s.

We give thanks for the guidance and wisdom of the elderly and the energy and enthusiasm of young people, we pray they experience the respect and admiration they deserve. **Lord hear us**.

We give thanks for the gifts of life, food, shelter, education and friendship, we pray that we may always appreciate all we have. **Lord hear us**.

Let us pray.

For what has been in our lives, Lord God, we say thanks; for what is to come, we say yes. Make us people of gratitude and hope all the days of our life. We make our prayer through Christ our Lord. Amen.

PRAYER OVER THE GIFTS

Lord, we offer you our bread and wine,
and with them we give you thanks
for all that is good in our lives,

especially our faith in Jesus Christ,
for he gives meaning to our lives.
We make this prayer through Christ our Lord. Amen.

REFLECTION

Dear God, as I arise today:I give thanks for the gift of life, that I can enjoy every day to the full.
I give thanks for the gift of hearing, that I can appreciate the goodness of others.
I give thanks for the gift of sight, that I can admire the beauty of creation.
I give thanks for the gift of touch, that I can feel both sunshine and rain.
I give thanks for the gift of speech, help me to use it to spread kindness and positivity.
I give thanks for the education that is available to me so that I can reach my potential.
I give thanks for the food that nourishes me every day.
I give thanks for the talents with which I have be gifted, help me to be confident in using them.
I give thanks for the roof over my head and floor under my feet when I wake to greet each new day, help to me to mindful of those who do not.
I give thanks for second chances and opportunities to make amends to those who I have hurt.
I give thanks for the love shown to me by those around me, help me to show affection in return.
I am grateful for all that I have, help me to appreciate all that I have and not to get distracted in chasing the things that I don't.
I am blessed. Amen.

or

When you say thanks, you grow a little;
thanks is like food for the heart and soul.
We're thankful for a compliment,
for help with study,
for advice with a problem,
for good conversation:
when we're grateful,

we know we depend on others
for most of the good things of life,
and we can't go it alone.
Think for a moment of something you're thankful foror someone you feel gratitude towards;
allow yourself feel the thanks in your heart......
Doesn't it make you feel good?
You feel a bit humble,
joyful, excited,
and you feel you're in one piece.
And thanks to God.
Think of your thanks to God:
maybe for your faith, your health,
but above all for yourself.
Be grateful this moment
for who you are,
for the friendships in life,
and for the faith you have in God.

CONCLUDING PRAYER

Lord God, we go from this place
in thanks for your interest in us.
Make us people who are truly grateful
for the wonders of life,
and for strength and support
in times that are difficult.
Help us be more mindful, more grateful and more kind.
We make this prayer through Christ our Lord. Amen.

14. SELF-IMAGE

PREPARATION

In preparation the young people may spend some time reflecting on how they see themselves and the search for meaning in their lives. They may like to create a piece of art which reflects their positive characteristics and talents. A powerpoint presentation or video could be created to highlight all the talents among the young people in the group and any positive work they have been involved in. Different types of mirrors, maybe even a cracked mirror might be used to highlight how we see ourselves in different ways and how reality can be distorted depending on how we are feeling at the time or what we have been damaged by. The focus could also be on friendship and what it means to them.

INTRODUCTION

We all go through times of feeling good and bad about ourselves. You can sometimes feel like you're in a 'hall of mirrors' – look one way and you're fat, another and you're thin, another and you're tall. Everywhere you look, you look different. Our view of reality can be sometimes distorted and upsetting. Most of us feel different with different people, maybe shy with adults and confident with peers or vice versa. We have a sense of our value and loveableness when we're with a friend, and with someone else we can feel very inferior. We are often hurt by comments on social media or we strive for the perfect image. We wonder which is the 'real me', and it's important that we find out. In our search for meaning, our search to find out who we are and who we are to become, we find ourselves looking for answers that are not always easy to find.

The key word for our relationship with Jesus is friendship: friendship gives us a good sense of ourselves. That's what God wants in his relationship with us. We'll pray that we can see ourselves as God sees us, and treat each other like that: unique and individual, our differences deserving of respect.

PENITENTIAL RITE

We often need the friendship of Christ to let us know that we are loveable. We pray now, not just for forgiveness but for healing. We pray that Christ may let us know that he does love us, and that he can heal the memory of times in the past when our good sense of ourselves was damaged. We can be too critical and over-sensitive to what others say or do. Good friends accept us for who we are. Sometimes it takes other people to show us our positives. We are often embarrassed by compliments and shrug them off as untrue or impossible. Jesus accepts us as we are.

Lord Jesus, you have called us to be friends. **Lord have mercy**.

Christ our Lord, we are created by God in his image and likeness. **Christ have mercy**.

Lord Jesus, we believe in the goodness of everyone. **Lord have mercy**.

OPENING PRAYER

God, Father, you are the source of all life,
and the source of all love.
You have created and formed each person here
with the loving hand of care and the caring heart of friendship.
We ask you now to strengthen our belief
in the value and worth we each have in your sight.
We ask this through Jesus the Lord. Amen.

FIRST READING

Jeremiah 31:3, 33

God promised each of us everlasting love.

A reading from the prophet Jermiah.

The Lord says: I have loved you with an everlasting love and so I still maintain my faithful love for you. Look, the days are coming, when I shall make a new covenant with the people. Then I shall be their God and they will be my people. The word of the Lord.

RESPONSORIAL PSALM

Psalm 139

A poem about God's knowing each of us.

Response: I thank you for the wonder of my being.

It was you who created my being,
knit me together in my mother's womb.
I thank you for the wonder of my being,
for the wonders of all your creation. **R.**
Already you knew my soul,
my body held no secret from you,
when I was being fashioned in secret
and moulded in the depths of the earth. **R.**
O search me, God, and know my heart.
O test me and know my thoughts.
See that I follow not the wrong path
and lead me in the path of life eternal. **R.**

GOSPEL READING

Luke 5:1-11

Peter had an experience of different sides of himself when he met Jesus and for a while he thought he was 'all bad'. In that very moment Jesus saw other sides to him, and in both the good and bad sides of him that he saw, he called him as an apostles.

A reading from the holy Gospel according to Luke.

Jesus was standing one day by the lake of Gennesaret, with the crowd pressing around him listening to the word of God, when he caught sight of two boats close to the bank. The fishermen had gone out of them and were washing their nets. He got into one of the boats – it was Simon's – and asked him to put out a little from the shore. Then he sat down and taught the crowds from the boat.

When he had finished speaking he said to Simon, 'Put out into deep water and pay out your nets for a catch.' 'Master,' Simon replied 'we worked hard all night long and caught nothing, but if you say so, I will pay out the nets.' And when they had done this they netted such a huge number of fish that their nets began to tear, so they signalled to their companions in the other boats to come and help them; when these came, they filled the two boats to sinking point.

When Simon Peter saw this he fell at the knees of Jesus saying, 'Leave me, Lord; I am a sinful man.' But Jesus said to Simon, 'Do not be afraid; from now on it is people you will catch.' Then, bringing their boats back to land, they left everything and followed him.

The Gospel of the Lord.

PRAYER OF THE FAITHFUL

We pray now for a good sense of ourselves, help us to accept ourselves as we are.

Response: Lord, in your goodness, hear our prayer.

We pray especially for people who suffer a lot in life because they see themselves as of little value. **R.**

Help each person here, Lord, to see himself or herself reflected in your eyes, as you see us as infinitely loveable in your sight. **R.**

Lord, don't let our insecurities, guilt and our failures block us from believing in your love and acceptance of ourselves. **R.**

We remember people, especially young people, who make poor choices that allow them to avoid reality because their image of themselves is distorted. Lord, may we try in our friendships to give others a good sense of themselves. **R.**

Let us pray.

God, Father and friend, we pray that nothing in us will prevent us knowing that you are one who loves us. Help us make friendships where we accept each other. This we ask through Jesus Christ, our Lord. Amen.

PRAYER OVER THE GIFTS

We offer to you God, Creator and friend,
all the good desires of our lives.
We want to be people who can love as you love,
who can see in each of us here
a reflection of yourself and your love.
We make our prayer through Christ our Lord. Amen.

REFLECTION

I often wonder which is the real me:
the super confident talker with some people,
the shy, inferior self I find with others
or the carefree, generous self at another time?
Which 'me' do I bring to God?
The confident or the guilty?
My 'self' can be like a sky I wander in,
cloudy one day, bright another.
Which is the real me?
I am a mixture of different moods and thoughts,
changing views of myself and opinions of others.
God tells me that every hair on my head has been counted
and that there is no need to be afraid.
Lord, help me believe that this is the 'me' that you love,
that you say 'friend' to everything that is me.
Bless us, God our Father, as we leave this gathering.

or

You can be more than you dreamed....
Believe that you are far more wonderful than you ever dared imagine...
because you are.
Believe that you can be more than you could ever dream...because you can.
Believe that you have more courage than you can think...because you do.
Believe that you are stronger than you fears have allowed you to know... because you are.
Believe that you are able to love more fully than you ever thought possible... because you are able to.
Believe that you are unique in ways that you have never allowed yourself to acknowledge...because you are.
Believe it...if it's the last thing you do.
Believe it...because it's true.
May we know that you are close to us in love and friendship,
affirming what is good in us and calling us
into a life of friendship and love with you.

May we give to others a true sense of their own value.
We ask this in the name of Jesus the Lord. Amen.

(Joy Mitchell)

CONCLUDING PRAYER

May we know that you are close to us in love and friendship,
affirming what is good in us and calling us
into a life of friendship and love with you.
May we give to others a true sense of their own value.
We ask this in the name of Jesus the Lord.

15. SELF-ACCEPTANCE

PREPARATION

In preparation the young people may spend some time reflecting on their names, their unique talents and their likes and dislikes. Why is our name important to us and what does Isaiah means when he says 'I have called you by name'? What did Peter experience when Jesus called him? They may like to create a piece of art using the letters of their name to reflect their positive traits. They can use pictures, doodles or symbols and their work could be used to decorate the altar. A powerpoint presentation or video could be created and used to highlight all the talents of the young people in the group and any positive work they have been involved in.

INTRODUCTION

When we look at ourselves and think about what sort of people we are, we know we have qualities we like and qualities we don't like. We can be discouraged at times because we don't like who we are. At other times we feel very confident, joyful at who we are, especially when someone else accepts us easily.

We are often impatient; we want to be strong overnight, make relationships quickly, achieve success easily. But the best things in life grow slowly, and with some fits and starts. We sometimes learn by making mistakes. That's all part of what we'll pray over now, and we hope that by listening to a message of hope and confidence about ourselves, we'll be less hard on ourselves and on others.

PENITENTIAL RITE

We're often very impatient with the type of people we are; we want to be different and better. The gospel of Jesus invites us always to become stronger in love, but it also invites us to be patient with ourselves and with others. So we pray now, asking God's forgiveness for our selfishness and our impatience with others:

Lord Jesus, you grew in wisdom and in humanity. **Lord have mercy**.
Lord Jesus, you were patient with the faults of others. **Christ have mercy**.
Lord Jesus, you are our hope and our joy with God our Father. **Lord have mercy**.

OPENING PRAYER

We ask you, Lord,
that the strength of our personalities
be nourished and grow in our relationships with each other,
and that our faults and weaknesses also be used in your service.
Help us to be humble and sincere in our attitudes to others,
not intolerant and critical.
This we ask through Christ our Lord. Amen.

FIRST READING

Isaiah 43:1-7

In this Scripture God simply tells us that we are precious to him, that he loves us and knows us by name. Maybe this love from him will give us confidence in ourselves. No matter how insecure you may feel, God still loves you.

A reading from the prophet Isaiah.

Do not be afraid, for I have redeemed you;
I have called you by your name, you are mine.
Should you pass through the sea, I will be with you;
or through rivers, they will not swallow you up.
Should you walk through fire, you will not be scorched
and the flames will not burn you.
For I am your God,
the Holy One of Israel, your saviour.
You are precious in my eyes,
you are honoured and I love you.
Do not be afraid, for I am with you.

The word of the Lord.

RESPONSORIAL PSALM

Psalm 139

A poem of joy in accepting oneself.

Response: I thank you for the wonder of my being.

O Lord, you search me and you know me,
you know my resting and my rising,
you discern my purpose from afar.
You mark when I walk or lie down,
all my ways lie open to you. **R.**
For it was you who created my being,
knit me together in my mother's womb.
I thank you for the wonder of my being,
for the wonders of all your creation. **R.**

GOSPEL READING

Mark 3: 13-19

Jesus chose his apostles very carefully, he chose to call ordinary, hardworking people who had different life experiences and came from a variety of backgrounds. Those who heard their name being called followed because they were accepted for who they were. Our gospel reading today tells us about the mission of Jesus – what it was that he tried to do. As we listen to the words of the gospel, we might ask ourselves, as followers of Jesus, what is our mission today?

A reading from the holy Gospel according to Mark.

He now went up onto the mountain and summoned those he wanted. So they came to him and he appointed twelve; they were to be his companions and to be sent out to proclaim the message, with power to drive out devils. And so he appointed the Twelve, Simon to whom he gave the name Peter, James the son of Zebedee and John the brother of James, to whom he gave the name Boanerges or ‹Sons of Thunder›; Andrew, Philip, Bartholomew, Matthew, Thomas, James the son of Alphaeus, Thaddaeus, Simon the Zealot and Judas Iscariot, the man who was to betray him.

The Gospel of the Lord.

PRAYER OF THE FAITHFUL

Let's pray for our intentions and for the needs of the world as we see them.

Response: Lord, in your goodness, hear our prayer.

Give us patience, Lord, with how others grow and develop; let's not be over-critical of their weaknesses. **R.**

We pray for our parents and families. We know them well and experience so easily their good points and bad points. Help us to be understanding and kind. **R.**

For all those in our Church and in our world who are trying to ease famine, homelessness, unemployment in our times. May they not be discouraged by failure but encouraged by the good they do. **R.**

For those who are suffering due to illness, depression and self-doubt. May they find healing in the love, support and kindness of others. **R.**

For ourselves, that we may journey confidently and have belief in our ability to be a force for good in the world. **R.**

Let us pray.

Lord God, we thank you because you care for us, and love us. We ask that we can mirror your love in our acceptance of each other and our willingness to forgive. We ask this through Christ our Lord. Amen.

PRAYER OVER GIFTS

Accept our gift, Lord, we pray,
and give to us the friendship of Jesus, who has come among us
to be your love of the poor and the deprived in our world.
May our hearts be open in trust and in compassion
to spread your justice and love in our world.
We ask this in the name of Jesus the Lord. Amen.

REFLECTION

Just think, you're not here by chance, but by God's choosing. His hand formed you and made you the person you are. In creating you he compared you with no one else, you are one of a kind. You lack nothing that his grace cannot give you. He has allowed you to be here at this time in history to fulfil his special purpose for this generation.

(Roy Lessin)

or

Journey Confidently.

I am **B**eautiful: I am a unique person made in God's image with the potential to be great.

I am **E**ncouraging: I am a good friend, I watch my words, I have a kind heart and help others.

I am **L**oving and loved: I care about and respect those around me and am precious to those who love me.

I am **I**mpatient: I may not always say or do the right thing but I always do my best on a journey where I have many paths to choose from.

I am **E**xceptional: I have many talents and use the gifts with which I have been blessed for the good of others.

I am **F**aithful: I believe, aiming to follow the example of Jesus and other positive role models in word and action.

I am **A**ssured: I am optimistic, positive and courageous even when I am fearful.

I am **C**alm: I take time to be silent and breathe deeply, being mindful that my soul is nourished in moments of peace.

I am **C**hallenged: I am aware I may need to turn to others for help when I feel anxious, jealous, upset or confused.

I am **E**mpathetic: I am considerate, I can be fragile at times and deserve to be treated with the respect and tenderness I show others.

I am **P**rayerful: I give praise and thanks for all I have been given and seek comfort in times of stress.

I am **T**ruthful: I am honest, trustworthy and just. I highlight injustices and speak out on behalf of the weak and voiceless.

May the Lord guide and protect me on my journey through life and help me every day to accept and love myself as I am.

Affirmations could be read aloud as a group or by individuals, or might be printed on a card for use as a daily prayer and students encouraged to use them.

CONCLUDING PRAYER

We thank you, Lord, for the gift of Jesus, who is the meaning of our lives.

May our prayer together at this table give us a sense of our own goodness and a confidence to believe in all this and share it with others.

We ask this through Jesus who is Lord. Amen.

16. FORGIVENESS

PREPARATION

The group might gather stones and place them in a central place, symbols of what they need forgiveness for.

INTRODUCTION

We can all feel a sense of guilt before God at times. We may know why – perhaps because of ways we treated others or spoke about them. The God we meet in the gospel is one who forgives. He knows our weaknesses and the ways in which we feel we have let him down.

Sometimes we wonder what exactly sin is. Maybe a good word for it is meanness, like when we know that we have used someone else. This is what turning from God means.

What is often harder is to forgive ourselves. We remember for a long time ways in which we let others down or used them, cheated or were mean. The forgiveness of God can be a help to us to forgive ourselves. The certainty that he is forgiving can be a healing power for us and help us to look on ourselves with forgiveness and a new confidence. We will pray that we can know deeply in our hearts the forgiveness of God.

or

If you have ever experienced compassion you'll know that it is an essential part of any good relationship. In the family, in friendship and in love compassion is the ability to know deeply the joys and troubles of another and to enter into them.

You might sometimes ask yourself, 'What's really going on in the people I'm close to, my best friend, father, sister, mother, boy-friend, girl-friend?' We may live closely with people and be unaware of how they really are.

Compassion is like a key opening a stiff door: it invites you to be yourself and to share yourself, to experience that nobody is alone in the world and that joys and troubles shared are moments of grace and of growth. In the gospel Jesus is compassionate, he seems to have this exciting and gentle quality of feeling for those he meets and of acceptance for them. His own invitation to each of us is to be compassionate, an essential quality of a Christian. That's what we'll pray about today.

PENITENTIAL RITE

Lord, we have sinned against you. **Lord have mercy**.

Lord, you are kind and compassionate to all who call on you. **Christ have mercy**.

Lord, you are our reconciliation with God our Father. **Lord have mercy**.

OPENING PRAYER

We come to you, Father, with confidence
that you are forgiving and accepting of each of us.
Heal us so that we are more loving,
that we can forgive others
and allow your forgiveness to be a strength in our lives.
We ask this in the name of Jesus the Lord. Amen.

FIRST READING

Isaiah 1:16-18

The reading is about the forgiveness of sins. God's mercy puts the guilt and shame of a person's past where it should belong, in the past.

A reading from the prophet Isaiah.

Take your wrong doing out of my sight.
Cease to do evil.
Learn to do good, search for justice, help the oppressed,
be just to the orphan, plead for the widow.
Come now, let us talk this over, says the Lord.
Though your sins are like scarlet, they shall be as white as snow;
though they are red as crimson, they shall be like wool.

The word of the Lord.

RESPONSORIAL PSALM

Psalm 104

This is a poem celebrating that God is always forgiving us.

Response: Lord, you are kind and forgiving.

The Lord is compassion and love,
slow to anger and rich in mercy.
He does not treat us according to our sins
nor repay us according to our faults. **R.**
As a father has compassion on his children,
the Lord has pity on those who fear him.
As far as the east is from the west,
so far does he remove our sins. **R.**

GOSPEL READING

Luke 23:33-34, 39-43

The sign of the cross is a sign of Jesus' compassion: he could respond to the sufferings of others, even in his own suffering. He was concerned on Calvary for the thieves on either side of him, and for those who were killing him.

A reading from the holy Gospel according to Luke.

When they reached the place called The Skull, they crucified him there and the two criminals also, one on the right, the other on the left. Jesus said, 'Father, forgive them; they do not know what they are doing.' Then they cast lots to share out his clothing.

One of the criminals hanging there abused him. 'Are you not the Christ?' he said. 'Save yourself and us as well.' But the other spoke up and rebuked him, 'Have you no fear of God at all?' he said. 'You got the same sentence as he did, but in our case we deserved it: we are paying for what we did. But this man has done nothing wrong. Jesus,' he said, 'remember me when you come into your kingdom.'

'Indeed, I promise you,' he replied, 'today you will be with me in paradise.'

The Gospel of the Lord.

PRAYER OF THE FAITHFUL

We pray to God for our intentions after hearing his word about forgiveness.

Response: Lord in your compassion, hear our prayer.

We pray that we can be sensitive to how others find their lives, not judging people just by how they look; knowing that there is so much more going on than meets the eye. **R.**

We pray that all of us may have hearts like your Son's, open to the hopes and troubles of everyone we meet. **R.**

Let's pray that we may be people of forgiveness ourselves, knowing that we are forgiven by God. **R.**

We pray that knowledge of God's forgiveness will help us always to forgive ourselves when we feel guilt or shame. **R.**

We pray Lord for anyone who has hurt us, in our family, among our friends or in school and for people who have let us down. Bless them and show them your kindness, even when we feel bitter towards them. **R.**

Let us pray.

Lord God, may your example of forgiveness, shown in Jesus, help us forgive others.
We pray that your people everywhere may show
in their lives and relationships
the power and strength of forgiveness.
We ask this in the name of Jesus the Lord. Amen.

PRAYER OVER THE GIFTS

Lord God, we pray that through our offering of bread and wine,
and our welcoming of your Son Jesus into our liveswe may believe more fully in your forgiveness.
Help us to become people of forgiveness in our world,
in the friendship and justice of Jesus,
in whose name we pray.

REFLECTION

To forgive and be forgiven is to enter a world of freedom;
it's to be free of grudges and bitterness
which block and damage love within us,
like water hindered in its flow.
It's to be free of misjudging others
which can block the growth of friendship
as tangled roots hinder the growth of a tree.
To forgive is to share in the victory of the cross,
when Jesus forgave those who harmed him so much.
To forgive is to be strong enough
and to really believe
that the person is bigger than any actions.
To forgive is to grow
and to allow oneself to be forgiven is to grow also
into a deeper sharing in the forgiving love of God.

or

Why do we call Good Friday 'good'? Strange name when it is a day of violence, mockery, pain and torture. The worst of torture took place in Jesus' time, just as it does today. This is a day when we can reflect with feeling on the cruelty of child labour and of slavery, the injustice of the imprisonment of the innocent in our world and the violence and bullying that can take place, even within the family. Yet, we can still call it good! It is good because of God and because of love. It is good because of the forgiveness of God for you and me, for the evil and sin of the world. Today is good because it is a day of healing. A day when Jesus showed by example how we could live.

CONCLUDING PRAYER

We have received the forgiveness of your Son,
Lord God, in our sinfulness and sins.
We know you do not hold our past against us.
Help us, through this Eucharist,
to be people who offer to others
the forgiveness that is yours, in Jesus Christ our Lord. Amen.

17. CELEBRATING DIFFERENCES

PREPARATION

Schools today welcome students of different Christian denominations, other religious faiths and of different nationalities. Schools encourage students to grow in their own faith and religious practice while at the same time respecting the distinctive Catholic ethos of the school.

The theme of this liturgy is to celebrate the values of pluralism, multiculturalism, inclusion and cooperation within our school faith community.

A Motto

Students could explore the idea of composing a motto that could be displayed during the liturgy. For example: 'United in diversity' (the motto of the European Union) or 'Walk together. Work together. Love each other.' (Pope Francis) or 'The lamps are different but the light is the same'. These could be translated into the languages of the students and displayed in posters or banners in the prayer space.

Flags and National Emblems

Students could research the flags and national emblems of the various countries associated with members of the school community. Posters of these could be displayed in the prayer space or carried in the entrance procession.

Peace Tree

A large and attractive branch of a tree could be placed in the prayer space. During the liturgy students could be invited to hang pre-prepared religious symbols (of peace) from the various faith traditions on the branch.

INTRODUCTION

God has made all of us alike, yet different in so many ways. People in our school and in our community come from different backgrounds and cultures. Many of us have different customs and speak different languages. We may have different ideas about how to express our faith. Each and every one of us has a different way of reacting to any given situation. Today we celebrate our differences and our diversity. We show respect and friendship towards all those who have entered our lives and we accept them for who we all are – children of God.

PENITENTIAL RITE

Lord, you are the way that leads to the Father. **Lord, have mercy**.
Christ, you are the truth that brings affirmation and joy to the world. **Christ, have mercy**.
Lord, you are the life that renews the world. **Lord have mercy**.

OPENING PRAYER

God of Love, you created all people in your image. We thank you for the wonderful variety of races and cultures in this world. Enrich our lives through ever-widening circles of friendship, and show us your presence in those who differ most from us. We ask this through your Son, Jesus Christ our Lord. Amen.

FIRST READING

Galatians 3: 26-28

All are one in the mind of God.

A reading from the Book of Galatians.

> It is through faith that all of you are God's children in union with Christ Jesus. You were baptised into union with Christ, and now you are clothed, so to speak, with the life of Christ himself. So there is no difference between Jews and Gentiles, between slaves and free people, between men and women; you are all one in union with Christ Jesus.

The word of the Lord.

RESPONSORIAL PSALM

Psalm 67

All The Nations are called to bless God.

Response: let all the peoples praise the Lord our God.

Let the peoples praise you, O God;
let all the peoples praise you.
Let the nations be glad and sing for joy,
for you judge the peoples with justice
and guide the nations upon earth. **R.**
Let the peoples praise you, O God;
let all the peoples praise you.
May God continue to bless us;
let all the ends of the earth revere him. **R.**

GOSPEL READING

John 4: 3-15

In this reading, Jesus crosses barriers of culture, religion and gender, and in his meeting with the Samaritan woman there is a change in who gives and who receives, what is given and what is received, and what thirst is quenched. In this meeting new possibilities are revealed.

A reading from the holy Gospel according to John.

Jesus left Judea and went back to Galilee; on his way there he had to go through Samaria. In Samaria he came to a town named Sychar, which was not far from the field that Jacob had given to his son Joseph. Jacob's well was there, and Jesus, tired out by the trip, sat down by the well. It was about noon. A Samaritan woman came to draw some water, and Jesus said to her, 'Give me a drink of water.' The woman answered, 'You are a Jew, and I am a Samaritan – so how can you ask me for a drink?' (Jewish people would not use the same cups and bowls that Samaritans use.) Jesus answered, 'If you only knew what God gives and who it is that is asking you for a drink, you would ask him, and he would give you life-giving water.' 'Sir,' the woman said, 'give me that water! Then I will never be thirsty again, nor will I have to come here to draw water.'

The Gospel of the Lord.

PRAYER OF THE FAITHFUL

Let us offer our prayers and intention to God.

We pray for unity in our global human family, that we may work together to protect those who are most vulnerable and most in need in our own country and throughout the world. **Lord hear us**.

We pray for the openness and the grace to see every human being as a child of God, regardless of race, language or culture. **Lord hear us**.

We pray for all those who have experienced violence and racism in our own country and throughout the world. May they find healing and justice and be able to live in safety and love. **Lord hear us**.

We pray in thanks for the uniqueness of everyone here and in our school community. We pray that we may have the courage to accept our differences, the strength to resist our prejudice and the love to care for each other. **Lord hear us**.

Let us pray.

Be with us Lord as we make our prayers. Make us truly grateful for love and faith in our lives, and for our faith in you, the creator of all people. We make this prayer in the name of Jesus our Lord. Amen.

PRAYER OVER THE GIFTS

In bread and wine Lord God you unite us to the love of Jesus your Son. Unite your people of all nations, faiths and colour. Through Christ our Lord. Amen

REFLECTION

St Teresa's Prayer

(Sung or adapted to be read).

Christ has no Body now but yours
No hands, no feet on earth but yours
Yours are the eyes through which he looks
Compassion on this world

Yours are the feet with which he walks
To do good
Yours are the hands with which he blesses
All the world

Yours are the hands
Yours are the feet
Yours are the eyes
You are his Body

Christ has no Body now but yours
No hands, no feet on earth but yours
Yours are the eyes through which he looks
Compassion on this world
Christ has no body now on earth but yours.

or

For all those who see 'home'
and all it means
disappears behind then as they flee;
for all those who cannot see a home
in the days ahead of them;
for all who dwell in daily insecurity
in tents and camps;
For those who are weary and
without hope in the days ahead;
For all members of refugee
families we pray.
May the image of the holy family
fleeing oppression
stay with us as we pray
for your displaced children;
during the day,
and each night
as we are blessed
with returning to a home.

May we also be blessed
with compassion for those still weary,
still uprooted,
still far from home. Amen.

CONCLUDING PRAYER

Almighty God, through your Holy Spirit you created unity in the midst of diversity; we acknowledge that human differences are an expression of your love for your creation; empower us to recognise and celebrate difference as your great gift to all of us.

Enable us to show and celebrate our differences through understanding, respect and love. We ask this through Christ our Lord. Amen.

DIVERSITY BLESSING

May the God who created a world of diversity and vibrancy,
go with us as we embrace life in all its fullness.
May the Son who teaches us to care for strangers and foreigners,
go with us as we try to be good neighbours in our communities.
May the Spirit who breaks down our barriers and celebrates community,
go with us as we find the courage to create a place of welcome for all.

(Education for Justice)

18. THINK BIG

PREPARATION

To prepare for this liturgy students can cut out large think bubbles and inside them illustrate or write the dreams that they have for the world such as peace, homes for all, an end to hunger, a clean environment and their dreams for themselves. These can then be placed on the walls so that as students walk in, they will be surrounded by these 'big' ideals.

INTRODUCTION

We often wonder what life will bring. Life will be, as it is now, what we make of it. It will be what we settle for. Pope Francis says to young people, 'think big!' That's what Jesus invites us to do, and that is what Jesus did.

PENITENTIAL RITE

Have mercy on me, God, in your kindness. Cleanse me from sin. **Lord have mercy**.

Against you have I sinned, you love truth in the heart. **Christ have mercy**.

A pure heart create for me, O God, give me again the joy of your help; O rescue me, God, my helper. **Lord have mercy**.

OPENING PRAYER

Lord God, we bring you the dreams we have for our lives. Help us to want what you want for each of us and for our world. May we spread your good news wherever we are. We ask this through Christ our Lord. Amen.

FIRST READING

Jeremiah 29:11-14

The prophet Jeremiah writes about the importance of trust and hope in our lives for facing the future with confidence. They ensure a sense of wellbeing and happiness.

A reading from the prophet Jeremiah.

Yes, I know what plans I have in mind for you, Yahweh declares, plans for peace, not for disaster, to give you a future and a hope. When you call to me and come and pray to me, I shall listen to you. When you search for me, you will find me; when you search wholeheartedly for me, I shall let you find me…

The word of the Lord.

RESPONSORIAL PSALM

Psalm 8

The greatness of all God's creation.

Response: Glory and Praise to you O Lord.

When I see the heavens, the work of your hands,
the moon and the stars which you arranged,
what is man that you should keep him in mind,
the son of man that you care for him? **R.**
Yet you have made him little lower than the angels;
with glory and honor you crowned him,
gave him power over the works of your hands:
you put all things under his feet. **R.**

GOSPEL READING

Matthew 9: 35-38

There is much to be done. Jesus saw that too. He invited people into his big harvest.

A reading from the Gospel of Matthew.

Jesus made a tour through all the towns and villages, teaching in their synagogues, proclaiming the good news of the kingdom and curing all kinds of diseases and sickness. And when he saw the crowds he felt sorry for them because they were harassed and dejected, like sheep without a shepherd. Then he said to his disciples, 'The harvest is rich but the labourers are few, so ask the Lord of the harvest to send labourers to his harvest'.

The Gospel of the Lord.

PRAYER OF THE FAITHFUL

Let us offer prayers and intentions to God in the name of Jesus, who cares for his people.

We pray that we can believe in our own goodness and the goodness of everyone. **Lord hear us**.

We pray that we can be helpers to people of need in our school and neighbourhood. **Lord hear us**.

We pray for all who care for the poor and the needy in our localities. **Lord hear us**.

We pray for the sick, especially in our families. **Lord hear us**.

Let us pray.

Hear our prayers O Lord, and give us a strong belief in the goodness of us all. Help us also encourage others to think big in their lives, we ask this through Christ our Lord. Amen.

PRAYER OVER GIFTS

Enlarge our willingness, O Lord, to be people active and committed in your service. Through Christ our Lord. Amen.

REFLECTION

Thinking big includes others in our decisions.

It means we want to make a difference to the lives of others, especially of the poor.

It means taking ourselves as we are and knowing we can be a means of goodness and justice in the world.

It means believing in ourselves and in God who creates us every day.

Thinking big will make a difference: let's believe we can make a difference.

CONCLUDING PRAYER

Let us pray.

God, creator and lover of all you see, thank you for the big desire we have to make a difference in the world. Thank you too for the people who have helped us have big desires, because they thought big. Thank you for the help you give us to think big, and to share in the big work of Jesus your Son. Amen.

19. CARE FOR THE EARTH

PREPARATION

The following symbols could be used.

A seed box: the seeds here are invisible to the eye. We know, however, that these seeds will grow through the gifts of soil, light and water. May we always remember the need to care for creation.

Two bottles (one an example of polluted water and the other an example of clean water): we look at the difference between these bottles and ask the question what type of Earth do we want to live in today? We ask for God's help to understand how to care for the earth.

Two flower boxes (the first shows us an example of withered plants, the other, plants in full flower): which of these flower boxes gives us great joy and which gives us sadness? We ask for God's help to understand how to care for the earth.

Gardening gloves, a shovel and material from the Green School Committee: may God bless the work of all people who care for our earth.

INTRODUCTION

The theme of our Eucharist today is 'the Gift of the Earth'. Every day we hear reports of how our human family is failing to care for the Earth. We hear about the melting of the polar caps, th expansion of the deserts, the pollution of the rivers and seas and other chronicles of the Earth's destruction. Today we remember that the Earth is not a resource with which to make profit but a resource to fulfil the needs of all. It is a gift of God.

PENITENTIAL RITE

As we call to mind the value God has for all living creatures, we acknowledge that we have sinned and added to the pollution of our earthly home through our failures to act responsibility.

God our Creator, forgive us for the times we have littered our earthly home. **Lord have mercy**.

God our Creator, forgive us for the times we have hoarded and not shared with people in need. **Christ have mercy**.

God our Creator, enlighten our lives with your vision for the Earth so that we all share in the fullness of life. **Lord have mercy**.

OPENING PRAYER

Lord God, you created everything and you saw that it was good.
Help us to care for what you have made,
for the Earth, for our rivers, for our beaches,
for all the resources of the Earth,
and to use them that all may live in dignity and in safety.
We ask this through Christ our Lord. Amen.

FIRST READING

Ecclesiasticus 43:13

This is a song of praise to God for all he has made. When we praise him for the Earth and the whole world, we can ask ourselves how we, his people, use the Earth.

A reading from the book of Ecclesiasticus.

Praise the Lord, my soul,
Lord my God, how great you are!
Clothed in majesty and splendour,
wearing the light as a robe.
You fixed the earth on its foundations;
in the ravines you opened up springs,
running down between the mountains;
from your high halls you water the mountains,
satisfying the earth with the fruit of your works:
for cattle you make the grass grow,
and for people the plants they need,
to bring forth food from the earth,
food to make them sturdy of heart.
How countless are your works, O Lord,
all of them made so wisely.

The word of the Lord.

RESONSORIAL PSALM

Psalm 147

Praise to God for creation.

Response: We praise you, O God, our creator.

Sing to the Lord with thanksgiving;
make melody to our God on the lyre!
He covers the heavens with clouds;
he prepares rain for the earth;
he makes grass grow on the hills. **R.**
He makes peace in your borders;
he fills you with the finest of the wheat.
He sends out his command to the earth;
his word runs swiftly.
He gives snow like wool;
he scatters frost like ashes. **R.**

GOSPEL READING

John 1:1-2.

Everything was created by the word of God. All creation demands our respect.

A reading from the holy Gospel according to John.

In the beginning was the Word: the Word was with God and the Word was God. He was with God in the beginning. Through him all things came into being, not one thing came into being except through him. What has come into being in him was life, life that was the light of all; and light shines in darkness, and darkness could not overpower it.

The Gospel of the Lord.

PRAYER OF THE FAITHFUL

Let us pray to God, creator of all that is, for our intentions.

Response: Creator Lord, hear our prayer.

We present our prayer to our God; Father, Son and Holy Spirit, who has gifted us Earth as your common home, so that we may live abundantly. **R.**

We pray that world leaders recognise our dependence on the planet and therefore our need to care for it. May they find ways forward for all to contribute to care for our planet, and make it sustainable for the future. We pray to the Lord. **R.**

We pray that we seek ways to establish social and economic justice to overcome the immense poverty and inequality in our world. God has provided us with resources for our needs, not our greed. We pray to the Lord. **R.**

We pray that our school community may understand the need for change to sustain the Earth for all. In understanding these issues, may we commit ourselves to making a difference to our world. We pray to the Lord. **R.**

We pray as a community, remembering our parents, grandparents and all who share in our lives. We ask God for the strength to support all who care for us. We pray to the Lord. **R.**

We pray for all gathered here. We ask God to hear our worries and concerns.

Let us pause to silently pray for any special needs of our own. We pray to the Lord. **R.**

Let us pray.

God our creator, you see all you have created and see that it is good. Help us always to respect the goodness of your creation. We aks this through Christ our Lord. Amen.

PRAYER OVER THE GIFTS

Lord God, from the many gifts you give us, we place this bread and wine on your altar.

We know that many people badly need ordinary food and drink.

Make us caring people like your Son, Jesus Christ our Lord. Amen.

REFLECTION

A Prayer for the Earth – Taken from *Laudato Si.*

All-powerful God, you are present in the whole universe

and in the smallest of your creatures. You embrace with your tenderness all that exists. Pour out upon us the power of your love,

that we may protect life and beauty. Fill us with peace that we may live
as brothers and sisters, harming no one.
O God of the poor,
Help us to rescue the abandoned and forgotten of the Earth, so precious in your eyes.
Bring healing to our lives,
that we may protect the world and not prey on it, that we may sow beauty, not pollution and destruction.
Touch the hearts of those who look only for gain at the expense of the poor and the Earth.
Teach us to discover the worth of each thing,
To be filled with awe and contemplation, to recognise that we are profoundly united with every creature, as we journey towards your infinite light.
We thank you for being with us each day.
Encourage us, we pray, in our struggle for justice, love and peace.
Amen.

or

Let there be respect for the Earth.
Peace for its people.
Love in our lives.
Delight in the good.
Forgiveness for past wrongs
and from now on a new start.
Amen.

or

'There lives the dearest freshness deepdown things.' (Gerard Manley Hopkins)
What would come to mind?
A daffodil blowing in the wind?
A feather caught in the gate of a sheepfold?
Earth, damp and strong?
And you feel you're part of all God's creation
and all is very good.
A joy to believe in God the Creator,
a joy to partake in creation:

a child's first smile,
an old man's gentle hardworked hand,
the air you breathe,
the water that refreshes:
the peace of God,
the life of Christ,
the joy of the Spirit.
'There lives the dearest freshness deepdown things'.
What else might come to mind?
The smog that darkens a city,
the river polluted and fish killed,
the burns of war on a child's back,
the young man or girl near the bomb at the wrong time,
the garden vandalised just for the hell of it?
And you dread being part of all that,
part of the destruction of what God has planned,
all that is very good is for our stewarding.
Father, forgive the violence that shatters your peace;
Jesus, forgive our neglect of life,
Spirit, forgive the destruction of beauty that we cause.
Father, thank you for the peace of your creation,
Jesus, thank you for the life you bring,
Spirit, thank you for the beauty of your life.

CONCLUDING PRAYER

As we leave today from this table of communion, may our hearts be on fire with your loving vision for our Planet Earth. May our giftedness help care for the Earth and for all who we meet today. We ask this through Christ our Lord. Amen.

20. JUSTICE

PREPARATION

This prayer service for justice can be celebrated at any time of the year, but may be particularly suitable during Lent. In preparation students could be encouraged to reflect on 'Living Lent' and putting faith into action. Students could be asked to decide on one action they could do for others during Lent to promote justice in their community, country or the world. They could write this action as a pledge on individual (credit card sized) 'pledge cards'. These cards could either be displayed during the service or included as part of the entrance procession.

INTRODUCTION

One of the clearest and most holistic words for justice in the Bible is the Hebrew word *Shalom* which means both justice and peace. *Shalom* includes 'wholeness' or everything that makes for people's wellbeing, and in particular, the restoration of relationships that have been broken.

Justice, therefore, is about repairing broken relationships both with other people and with structures in our society and in the world.

This presents a challenge for all of us in defending the dignity of each and every human being, promoting community and the common good and putting the needs of the poor and the vulnerable first.

That's the theme of our reflection and prayer today. What can we do to bring about justice and to help restore relationships in our world today? *Shalom!*

PENITENTIAL RITE

Often we see injustice but fail to act. We ask forgiveness for our failures and the failures of our world, forgiveness for when our actions or lack of action caused so much pain and hopelessness, hunger and homelessness, for so many people.

Lord Jesus, you said that what we do for our brothers and sisters on earth, we do for you. **Lord, have mercy**.

Lord Jesus, you are the truth which enlightens the nations. **Christ have mercy**.
Lord Jesus, you have come that we may have life and have it to the full. **Lord have mercy**.

OPENING PRAYER

Lord God, we pray that you may be a light in the darkness of injustice in our world:
we ask you that in the light you share with us,
we become more aware of the needs of your people:
see the faces stained by frustration; feel the thirst for justice;
and have the strength and courage to act for others.
We make this prayer through Christ our Lord. Amen.

FIRST READING

Micah 6:8

The prophet Micah was a simple man from the countryside who was not involved in power, law or politics. He identified with the poor, the powerless, the vulnerable and with the voiceless. In this short reading, he reveals how God wants us to live.

A reading from the prophet Micah.

No, the Lord has told us what is good. What he requires of us is this: to do what is just, to show constant love, and to live in humble fellowship with our God.

The word of the Lord.

RESPONSORIAL PSALM

Psalm 33

The Lord cares for the poor.

Response: The Lord hears the cry of the poor.

I will bless the Lord at all times,
his praise always on my lips;
in the Lord my soul shall make its boast.
The humble shall hear and be glad. **R.**
Look towards him and be radiant;

let your faces not be abashed.
This poor man called, the Lord heard him
and rescued him from all his distress. **R.**

GOSPEL READING

Luke 4:16-19

Our gospel reading today tells us about the mission of Jesus – what it was that he tried to do. As we listen we might ask ourselves, what is our mission today?

A reading from the holy Gospel according to Luke.

Then Jesus went to Nazareth, where he had been brought up, and on the Sabbath he went as usual to the synagogue. He stood up to read the Scriptures and was handed the book of the prophet Isaiah. He unrolled the scroll and found the place where it is written,

'The Spirit of the Lord is upon me,
because he has chosen me to bring good news to the poor.
He has sent me to proclaim liberty to the captives
and recovery of sight to the blind,
to set free the oppressed and announce that the time has come when the Lord will save his people.'

The Gospel of the Lord.

PRAYERS OF THE FAITHFUL

Now let us, as a community of faith, surround in prayer all those who are struggling because of injustice in today's world.

Response: God of justice, hear our prayer.

We pray today for people in the developing world who suffer because of the injustice of climate change, famine, corruption, violence and war. We ask that the selfishness and greed of the few be transformed into compassion and justice for the many. **R.**

We pray for the men, women and children who are without a home in our own country and throughout the world. We pray that they find the shelter, warmth, love and care that we associate with a home. **R.**

We pray for the poor and the vulnerable in our society: people who struggle with addiction, families who find it hard to make ends meet and those who are forced to live in poverty and despair. We pray that these people find hope in their lives and an ease to their pain. **R.**

We pray for our elected leaders and all those who hold power over others. We pray they be guided by the mission of Jesus, and will strive to continually work for a more equal and just society. **R.**

We pray for all those who feel victimised and imprisoned: those who experience racism and discrimination, who are bullied or suffer from mental illness. We ask that they have the courage and strength to ask for help and find relief and comfort from their suffering. **R.**

And finally, we pray for everyone here and in our school community. We pray that we will have the courage to use our voices and actions to bring about justice and live as men and women for others. **R.**

Let us pray.

God of Justice, we lift up all these prayers to you in the knowledge that you are already at work amid the brokenness of our lives, our relationships and our world and that you invite each of us to be a part of your holy work of justice. We offer to you these prayers today that you may call us to reflect your compassion, mercy and justice in all that we do. In your name we pray. Amen.

PRAYER OVER THE GIFTS

God of love and justice, accept these gifts, and with them our lives, to be used in your service; through Jesus Christ our Lord. Amen.

REFLECTION

When I was hungry you gave me food
and when I was thirsty you refreshed me;
I was lonely and you gave me your time,
homeless and you tried to put a roof over my head;
I was the victim of violence and greed and you fought for my rights,
I was a refugee and you took me in.
'When, Lord?, when?' we will say,
because we never see you, nor do we know you suffer still.
We wonder at so much inequality in the world

and it makes us angry, frustrated, helpless.
Sometimes you don't seem to be of much help,
remote, outside it all, and we say,
'Why didn't you make it all different?'
'When, Lord, when?' we will say,
and all you say, with a tear in your voice and hope in your heart,
'What you did for them, you did for me'.

or

You asked for my hands that you might use them for your purpose.
I gave them for a moment, then withdrew them, for the work was hard.
You asked for my mouth to speak out against injustice;
I gave you a whisper that I might not be accused.
You asked for my eyes to see the pain of poverty;
I closed them, for I did not want to see.
You asked for my life that you might work through me.
I gave a small part, that I might not get 'too involved'.
Lord forgive me for my calculated efforts to serve you
only when it is convenient for me to do so,
only in those places where it is safe to do so and
only with those who make it easy to do so.
Father, forgive me, renew me, send me out as a usable instrument
that I might take seriously the meaning of your cross.

(A prayer from Africa – Joe Seremane, South Africa)

CONCLUDING PRAYER

Thank you, Lord, for your presence with us this day. As we depart from this space now we want to see justice run like a river, bringing healing and peace in our world.

We want to be able to see clearly,
to act justly,
to live kindly,
to walk humbly,
to serve gratefully.
We ask this through Christ our Lord. Amen.